The Political Novel

DOUBLEDAY SHORT STUDIES IN POLITICAL SCIENCE

Consulting Editor
Richard C. Snyder
Associate Professor of Politics, Princeton University

The Revolution in American Foreign Policy, 1945–1954
By William G. Carleton, Professor of Political Science and Head Professor of the Social Sciences, University of Florida

Political Community at the International Level: Problems of Definition and Measurement
By Karl W. Deutsch, Professor of History and Political Science, Massachusetts Institute of Technology

France: Keystone of Western Defense
By Edgar S. Furniss, Jr., Assistant Professor of Politics, Princeton University

The Problem of Internal Security in Great Britain, 1948–1953
By H. H. Wilson, Associate Professor of Politics, Princeton University *and* Harvey Glickman, Fellow, Harvard University

Germany: Dilemma for American Foreign Policy
By Otto Butz, Assistant Professor of Political Science, Swarthmore College

The Role of the Military in American Foreign Policy
By Burton M. Sapin, Research Assistant, Foreign Policy Analysis Project, Princeton University *and* Richard C. Snyder, Associate Professor of Politics, Princeton University

Democratic Rights Versus Communist Activity
By Thomas I. Cook, Professor of Political Science, The Johns Hopkins University

The Social Background of Political Decision-Makers
By Donald R. Matthews, Assistant Professor of Government, Smith College

Readings in Game Theory and Political Behavior
By Martin Shubik, Research Associate, Economic Analysis Project, Princeton University

The American Vice-Presidency: New Look
By Irving G. Williams, Associate Professor and Chairman, Departments of History and Social Studies, St. John's University

Contemporary International Law: A Balance Sheet
By Quincy Wright, Professor of International Law, University of Chicago

Modern Colonialism: Institutions and Policies
By Thomas R. Adam, Professor of Political Science, New York University

Law as a Political Instrument
By Victor G. Rosenblum, Assistant Professor of Political Science, University of California, Berkeley

The Fate of the French Non-Communist Left
By E. Drexel Godfrey, Jr., Assistant Professor of Political Science, Williams College

The Political Process: Executive Bureau—Congressional Committee Relations
By J. Leiper Freeman, Assistant Professor and Research Associate, Graduate School of Education, Harvard University

German Political Theory, 1870 to the Present
By Otto Butz, Assistant Professor of Political Science, Swarthmore College

The Political Novel
By Joseph L. Blotner, Instructor in English, University of Idaho

Studies in Scope and Methods

The Study of Public Administration
By Dwight Waldo, Professor of Political Science, University of California, Berkeley

The Study of Political Theory
By Thomas P. Jenkin, Associate Professor and Chairman, Department of Political Science, University of California, Los Angeles

The Study of Comparative Government
By Roy C. Macridis, Associate Professor of Political Science, Northwestern University

Problems of Analyzing and Predicting Soviet Behavior
By John S. Reshetar, Jr., Lecturer in Politics, Princeton University

To order these titles and to receive forthcoming ones (none more than 95c), enter your subscription now. All titles will be sent on approval. COLLEGE DEPARTMENT, Doubleday & Company, Inc., 575 Madison Avenue, New York 22, N.Y.

Doubleday Short Studies in Political Science

The Political Novel

BY JOSEPH L. BLOTNER

University of Idaho

DOUBLEDAY & COMPANY, INC.

Garden City, N.Y.

1955

LIBRARY OF CONGRESS CATALOG CARD NUMBER 55–6672
PRINTED IN THE UNITED STATES OF AMERICA
AT THE COUNTRY LIFE PRESS, GARDEN CITY, N.Y.

Editor's Foreword

From time to time in the Doubleday Short Studies in Political Science series, guest analysts from outside the formal boundaries of the discipline will be invited to help fill certain gaps in existing materials. In the present instance a young professional student of literature, Dr. Joseph Blotner, has contributed a much-needed and highly useful introduction to the political novel. Thanks largely to the care and skill with which this analysis has been prepared, students of English and political science, as well as general readers, should find new and stimulating pathways open to them.

So far as the editor and author know, this is the first essay of its kind in the English language. The fact is worth noting because, despite the large number of political novels in all languages and despite the obvious importance of this particular species of the novel generally, scholars in the field of literature have not devoted systematic attention to it. Until Dr. Blotner decided to undertake a full-scale investigation of the political novel —of which the present essay is one of the beginning steps—the teacher of political science could search the modern language journals and literary periodicals in vain for help in canvassing the possibly valuable contributions of the novelist in describing and explaining political behavior.

The Political Novel is to be welcomed on still other grounds. It is interdisciplinary in scope and intent and it demonstrates anew the fruitful results which can be achieved when a scholar merges his technical competence in one branch of learning with his informed and enthusiastic interest in another. Moreover, crude and scattered though the bridges between pairs of the social sciences (e.g., political psychology) are, the bridges between the social sciences and the humanities are even more so. Collaboration—in this case between literature and political science—should certainly take more than one form, but whatever the form, the great need is to light up the shadowy twilight zones which lie between major disciplines. Not only are these unexplored areas of subject matter to be charted, there are common purposes and joint efforts to be considered. Among others, Dr. Blotner has raised the question: .what can the experts in literature and in politics give to each other?

The analysis of the political novel set forth in these pages makes a variety of contributions to learning. Novels can be read two ways: for pleasure and for profit. The latter object—as in all academic subjects—is sometimes pursued under conditions which deny the former. Nonetheless, the reader is reminded by Dr. Blotner that to be alerted beforehand to the nature and significance of this type of novel is to combine pleasure with an awareness that the content may be very revealing of data concerning political life. Thus the words of a writer are at once pleasure-giving and instructive—if the reader is looking out for the proper clues. Second, there is made available an original classification of political novels and politically relevant summaries to serve as a guide to political scientists. The bibliography, though selected, is especially useful in this respect. Third, the headings and substance of Chapters Two to Six actually provide a set of analytical functions which the author believes the novel may serve in illuminating major aspects of politics and government. This study is so cast that the transition from thinking about novels to thinking about politics is painless and without distortion. No one having any familiarity with the traditional categories of political science will find Dr. Blotner's own presentation strange or unsophisticated.

In addition, this essay represents an attempt to establish durable intellectual bases for probing the nature of the political novel. The tentative definitions and criteria of identification, classification of functions, and annotations are a substantial move in this direction. Finally, among the data revealed in the contents of political novels is evidence of the way a given society reacts to its own political institutions and practices. To the extent that such novels partially yet accurately reflect social reality, the student of politics can draw valid inferences concerning the political beliefs —including beliefs about the nature of politics—held by a sizeable portion of the society's membership at any one time. One can detect at least the broad outlines of periodic shifts in the political concerns of a people or any segment thereof in their literature.

Chapter One discusses some problems arising from a study of the political novel. This is an important chapter and contains some homely wisdom on the different approaches respectively of the novelist and the political scientist. It should be stressed that certain crucial points with respect to the analysis of human behavior in general can be raised by comparing the techniques of the two kinds of observers and reporters. The well-known remark about pictures being worth thousands of words has occasionally been transposed to the effect that one good story is worth a whole (and dry) textbook. This, of course, is an attractive argument. But it does raise the fundamental question of what analytical operations are performed by the novelist on the one hand and the political scientist on the other. Offhand it would seem as though there were important differences carrying beyond those of purposes discussed by the author. Generally speaking, the novelist is primarily concerned with a coherent story, with a whole fabric of description, and with specific details while the political scientist is concerned with events, processes, and factors, with abstractions from wholes and with classes of general phenomena. The latter builds upon numerous instances, upon gross data, and upon repeated patterns of behavior. The former builds upon an amassing of individualized data fashioned into a unique chronicle. The one gains richness and sacrifices capacity to generalize, the other sacrifices detail for broad generalization. For the novelist, Uncle Tom becomes a microcosm, a device for revealing the tragedy of the whole Negro race in America through a portrait of a single character. For the political scientist, Uncle Tom is lost in what can be said of the entire group of which he is a member. Both are limited and both pay a price accordingly. Clearly more is involved in the different analytic techniques but it suffices to indicate one type of issue raised in this study of the political novel.

Other issues are equally noteworthy. The main character in a novel may be likened to a dummy—or a model—created by the author for the purposes of expressing the author's observations and, in effect, for "playing out" his ideas. Though the character is pure fiction—i.e., any similarities to known real persons are coincidental—an effective novel must have *believable* characters, recognizable through behavior traits identified by readers from their own everyday experience. So too the social scientist uses models—analytic dummies—to further his purposes. Dissecting the anatomy of a political model and putting its characters under close examination can teach something about the most fruitful relationships between real persons and fictional characters for purposes of describing and explaining behavior. Often the fact that the novelist is actually building models is obscured by the amount of detail he pours into his molds which then makes his models seem remarkably lifelike. While the models of the social scientist are usually much further removed from correspondence to real persons, the properties built into them must be "believable" too.

Another area of inquiry can be opened up if one accepts the cues offered by Dr. Blotner's selections and analyses. Political novels seem to reflect mostly the seamy side of political life, emphasizing conflict as the sole theme meriting attention. Through their characters, authors seem to place great blame for social ills on political institutions as detached from other institutions or on individual devils. Is this a reliable and full revelation of politics? As a matter of fact, novels too seem caught in two opposite kinds of explanations: the great man and the great historical force. Each has significant limitations and accompanying fallacies yet each assumes great plausibility at the hands of a skillful storyteller. Inevitably the novelist dramatizes, and in real life the political actor dramatizes too. Unfortunately, the tendency to dramatize reinforces the neglect of the mundane factors which often influence crucial political action and choice.

This line of thought suggests certain concrete exercises which might be profitable for the student of politics to undertake. Since the search for fruitful hypotheses is a backbone of any systematic discipline, it might be useful to search these novels to see if any have been missed. A corollary effort would be to check the knowledge of politics exhibited in political novels against the latest agreements among political scientists. Still another effort might be directed toward a content analysis (in the technical sense) of the novel as medium of communication in order to throw light on the value structure of the society or individuals which are depicted. Finally, what aspects of politics have been ignored by novelists and why? For example, a novel might be an excellent way to illuminate the world of the decision-maker, the governor, the leader. Thus far, none has really done so.

Dr. Blotner is to be congratulated for aiding an important cause: the use of novels as a teaching device in political science courses. Those who have tried have been rewarded but have lacked an introductory essay and bibliographical guidance. Novels make points which can be made in no other way and in interesting fashion. The student's idea of the political realm and of approaches to its understanding will be enlarged by following the thoughtful guide presented below.

One considerable merit of this monograph is a lighter style than is normally characteristic of political science literature. Nonetheless, its intellectual quality will make the reader anticipate Dr. Blotner's larger study.

RICHARD C. SNYDER

Contents

Contents

chapter one

The Study of the Political Novel

The Importance of the Political Novel

In an age in which progressively more men have engaged in politics while the politics themselves have become increasingly complex, any means for understanding these interrelated phenomena becomes correspondingly more valuable. The techniques of science are constantly being brought to bear upon this problem of understanding. But one of the best means of enlightenment has been available for more than a hundred years. Since its beginning the political novel has fulfilled the ancient function of art. It has described and interpreted human experience, selectively taking the facts of existence and imposing order and form upon them in an esthetic pattern to make them meaningful. The political novel is important to the student of literature as one aspect of the art of fiction, just as is the psychological novel or the economic novel. But it is important in a larger context, too. The reader who wants a vivid record of past events, an insight into the nature of political beings, or a prediction of what lies ahead can find it in the political novel. As an art form and an analytical instrument, the political novel, now as ever before, offers the reader a means for understanding important aspects of the complex society in which he lives, as well as a record of how it evolved.

The Nature of the Political Novel: Problems of Definition and Selection

The political novel is hard to define. To confine it to activity in the houses of Congress or Parliament is to look at the top floor of the political structure and to ignore the main floor and basement which support it. One has to follow the novelist's characters on the stump and into committee rooms—sometimes even farther. But the line is drawn where the political element is forced into the background by the sociological or economic. The political milieu develops in part out of the conditions described in Upton Sinclair's The Jungle and John Steinbeck's The Grapes of Wrath. Although these books are proletarian novels, to include them would be to open the door to a flood of books that would spread far beyond the space limitations of this study. Of course, proletarian novels which are also political novels are included. Two such books are André Malraux's Man's Fate and Steinbeck's In Dubious Battle. But for the purposes of this study, a cast of characters drawn from the proletariat is not enough, even if they are oppressed economically and socially. They must carry out political acts or move in a

1

political environment. Also excluded are novels such as Herman Melville's
Mardi which treat politics allegorically or symbolically. Here a political
novel is taken to mean a book which directly describes, interprets, or
analyzes political phenomena.

Our prime material is the politician at work: legislating, campaigning,
mending political fences, building his career. Also relevant are the people
who influence him: his parents, his wife, his mistress, the girl who jilted
him, the lobbyist who courted his favor. The primary criterion for admis-
sion of a novel to this group was the portrayal of political acts, so many of
them that they formed the novel's main theme or, in some cases, a major
theme. These acts are not always obvious ones like legislating. In Joseph
Conrad's *Nostromo* a mine owner contributes financial support to political
movements which will provide a more favorable climate for his business.
In Dubious Battle presents labor organizers who manipulate a strike to
serve the political ends of the Communist Party. The terminology of the
theater can be helpful in bridging the gap between the world of actual
events and the world of fiction. It helps to show how various aspects of the
actual political process are translated into the forms of fiction. The author
may concentrate his attention upon the actors—the public officials who
make decisions and wield authority on behalf of the community or the
whole society. A good many of the actors may not be public officials, but
rather private citizens whose acts are political: voicing opinions, helping to
select candidates, voting, attempting to influence the political process, re-
volting. These actors, and those who are public officials, may demonstrate
factors in the overall drama which are predominantly political in their
consequences: attitudes, social power, social stratification. The novelist
will be concerned with the roles the actors play and the lines they speak,
the purposes they have and the strategies they employ. He may concentrate
upon the interaction between these actors or between them and the audience—the public. An author may choose to emphasize the drama as a whole
rather than the individual actors, highlighting the stage upon which it is
played out—the country or area of national life in which the scenes are
laid. This emphasis upon the drama will throw into sharp relief the events
and decisions in which the actors participate, and the framework of rules
or custom against which they take place.

The novels considered here deal with political activity at all levels—
local, state, national, and international. If, as von Clausewitz said, "War
is merely the continuation of Politics by other means," one may find
politics in war, too. This study, therefore, includes works on revolutionary
as well as parliamentary politics. On the international level especially one
encounters group attitudes which are politically relevant. The groups may
be the conventional social, economic, or political strata of British and
American society, or they may be those of the rigid Marxist state. Other
relevant attitudes spring from national characteristics, and many political
novels identify some of them. This definition is wide and inclusive, but so
is political activity.

The primary sources of this study are eighty-one political novels. Over half of them are by Americans. The next largest group is the work of English writers. Other novels are taken from Italian, French, German, Russian, and South African literature. These eighty-one novels are the minimum necessary to give an understanding of the political novel. At the same time, this is the maximum number that could be included in the study. Only in the case of the English and American political novel has an attempt been made to trace the development of literary genre. Some of these novels are used because they show artistic excellence, others because they show how the form developed historically. More American than English novels are used because they are more readily available, many of them in inexpensive, paper-bound editions. It was not possible to attempt the same outline with the other literatures because of the brevity of this study. For some of them, too, a sufficiently representative group of political novels was not available.

Most often the authors deal with their own countries, although they sometimes write about a foreign land. Some of them are hard to pigeon-hole: Henry James, an American expatriate writing about London terrorists in *The Princess Casamassima;* Joseph Conrad, an Anglicized Pole analyzing Russian revolutionaries in *Under Western Eyes;* Arthur Koestler, an Austrian-educated Hungarian living in France, describing the Moscow trials in *Darkness at Noon.* This is one reason why it is more fruitful for present purposes to avoid strict concentration on national literatures and to accept valid insights into national characteristics and behavior patterns no matter what the language of their source.

Characteristics of the Political Novel

In *The Charterhouse of Parma* the witty and urbane Stendhal says, "Politics in a work of literature are like a pistol-shot in the middle of a concert, something loud and vulgar yet a thing to which it is not possible to refuse one's attention." His own work contradicts the great French novelist, yet his comment is perfectly accurate for many other novelists. Politics in some modern novels of political corruption, such as Charles F. Coe's *Ashes,* do seem loud and vulgar, and in books like Upton Sinclair's the reader may hear not one pistol shot but a cannonade. But this is not to say that the use of political material must disrupt a work of literature. The trick, of course, is all in knowing how. Harriet Beecher Stowe wrote an artistically weak, politically successful work in *Uncle Tom's Cabin,* while Fyodor Dostoyevsky produced a politically unsuccessful, artistically enduring classic in *The Possessed.*

The quality of these novels varies widely, just as would that of a group dealing with religion, sex, or any other complex, controversial theme. In general, the European novels considered here attain a higher level than the American books. This is partly because only the better European novels are treated. But they are also superior to the best American works, except for a few comparatively recent ones, because of the wider variety of political experience presented, the greater concern with ideology and theory, and the deeper insight into individual motivation and behavior. This in turn is probably due to several factors. From the time when the United States attained its independence until the end of the first quarter of this century, it possessed a relatively stable set of doctrines and frames of reference (compared to those existing in Europe) within which the individual led his political life. Although American parties rose and declined, although the Union was preserved, its borders expanded, and international responsibility accepted, this evolution was orderly and limited compared to that which occurred in Europe. The Declaration of Independence, the Constitution, and the Bill of Rights provided a stable yet sufficiently flexible political framework. Europe during the same period reverberated with the French Revolution, the Napoleonic Wars, the unification of Germany and Italy, and the Russian Revolution. These were violent changes not only in theory but in the actual form of government. It is not unnatural then that American political novels range over a relatively narrower area, with their main emphasis on local or national subjects, while those of European authors delineate changing, conflicting, and radically different ideologies and resultant events. It is only since the 1930s, with the increase in centralized government, the impact of international Communism, and the recent appearance on both the Right and the Left of what seem to be threats to traditional American freedoms, that the American political novel has begun to approach the European in breadth of theme, concern with political theory, and interpretation of varying political behavior patterns.

The larger number of bad novels in the American group is also due to the fact that more American novels are treated. Because of their greater availability both for research and teaching, it is possible to show the evolution of this genre in the United States. In doing this one is able to examine the good ones, old and new, such as Henry Adam's *Democracy*, John Dos Passos' *District of Columbia* trilogy, and Irwin Shaw's *The Troubled Air*. One pays, however, by suffering through period pieces such as F. Marion Crawford's *An American Politician*. Less obtuse politically but nearly as abysmal artistically, is Paul Leicester Ford's *The Honorable Peter Stirling*. One is compensated, however, not only by the view of a developing genre, but also by the recording of significant periods in American national life and of the people who helped shape it, as in the Dos Passos work, and by the sensitive and penetrating analysis of central problems in contemporary life, as in Shaw's novel.

The English political novel is also uneven. That its depths are not so low as those in the American novel is due in part to the political heritage which its authors share with their colleagues on the continent. Its authors work from a long and rich political history in which the evolution has been less violent but no less steady.

The Novelist and the Political Scientist

The differences between the methods of the political novelist and the political scientist are worth studying. Their intentions are often at variance.

Whereas the scientist is dedicated to objectivity and statistical accuracy, the novelist is often consciously subjective; if his work is intended as a political instrument, as were *Uncle Tom's Cabin* and *The Possessed*, scrupulous attention to the claims of the other side will invariably lessen the emotional impact and political worth of the novel. If a scholar sets out to examine the rise of Nazism, he will have to treat not only the Beer Hall Putsch and the Reichstag fire, but German history and the German national character as well. He will chronicle the effects of Versailles, the staggering of the Weimar Republic, and the growing strength of the Brown Shirts. He will be concerned with national attitudes, with the relative strength of the parties that vied with the National Socialists. His study will gauge the effects of the aging Hindenburg and the demoniac Hitler on a people smarting from defeat, searching for a scapegoat, and longing for a resurgence. And all this will be backed with statistics where possible. It will be a cogently reasoned analysis with documented references to available sources. Also, the study will be aimed at a fairly homogeneous and well-defined audience. The appeal will be intellectual. If emotion creeps in, the work is probably bad.

The novelist who is to examine these same events will present them quite differently, even apart from the techniques of fiction. If he is a rather dispassionate chronicler of human foibles and frailties such as, say, Somerset Maugham, he will probably portray a group of people through whose actions the rise and significance of Nazism will become meaningful. The reader will probably observe the drifting war veteran, the hard-pressed workman, the anxious demagogue. Out of these lives and their interactions will emerge an objective study of the sources of a political movement and of the shape it took. If the novelist is an enthusiastic Nazi, the book will reflect his particular bias. The storm troopers will become heroic Horst Wessels, the young women stalwart Valkyries, the Führer an inspired prophet and leader. Out of the novel will come a plea for understanding or a justification of violence and a perverted view of German national destiny. The book will be emotionally charged, a calculated effort to produce a specific desired response. If this series of historical events is used by a Frenchman, they will undergo another change. There will probably be an evocation of the Junker mentality, of Prussian militarism, of hordes of gray-green figures under coal-scuttle helmets. If this novel is not a call to arms, it will be a warning cry to signal a growing danger. These three fictional books will use the same staples of the novelist's art, yet each will differ from the others in motivation and attitude. They will portray aspects of the same complex of events treated by the political scientist, but this will be virtually their only similarity.

A disadvantage for the novelist is his need to make his book appealing enough to sell and to make his reader want to buy his next novel. Although the scientist too must make his work as polished and interesting as he can, the novelist does not, like him, find his readers among subscribers to the learned journals. He cannot rely upon sales prompted by the need to keep abreast of research in a specialized field. If a novelist is to stay in print, political savoir-faire and intellectual capacity are not enough. He has to sell copies. Perhaps this is one reason why all but a few of these novels have a love story accompanying the political theme. Sometimes the love story inundates it, as in *An American Politician*; in other novels, such as Sinclair's *Presidential Agent*, it is peripheral and pieced out with flirtations. It may be that these novelists include this element because love is as much a part of life as politics. Its nearly universal presence is a reminder, however, of one aspect of the novelist's task and one way in which his work differs considerably from that of the political scientist.

The advantages of the novelist's method over the political scientist's compensate for the drawbacks. These advantages do not necessarily produce a better work, one which gives more insight into a problem or explains it better. They do, however, offer more latitude and fewer restrictions. The novelist may use all the techniques of the political scientist. Sinclair's *Boston* is studded with as many references to actual events, people, and documents as most scientific studies, although it is permeated by a violent partisanship which would make a scholarly study highly suspect. But this points up one of the novelist's advantages: he can use the methods of scholarship to document his case and then supplement them with heroes and villains who add an emotional appeal to the intellectual one. This string to the novelist's bow is a strong one. He can create a character like Shaw's Clement Archer in *The Troubled Air*, while the scientist is forced to use opinion research, carefully documented sources, and well-verified trends in treating the problem of deprivation of livelihood as a penalty for suspected political unreliability. Sometimes the scientist uses case histories, but the subjects are often identified by initials and treated with such antiseptic objectivity that almost no emotional impact comes through. The loss of Clement Archer's job, because he has employed actors blacklisted for suspected Communist activity by a newsletter acting as a self-appointed judge, presents this general problem with more frightening immediacy and reader-involvement than an excellent scholarly study could ever do. Archer becomes one embodiment of the problem—a rather naïve but courageous liberal made into a sacrificial goat because of his fight for what he believes to be traditional and critical American rights. If he wants to, the novelist can use historical personages to flesh out his story. Although the reader does not see him in its pages, Dos Passos' *The Grand Design* uses the figure of Franklin D. Roosevelt in the background as one of the mainsprings of the action. An individual may appear in transparent fictional guise. The *roman à clef* has many representatives in the political novel. Pyotr Verhovensky in Dostoyevsky's *The Possessed* has been identified as the revolutionary Sergei Nechaev. Hamer Shawcross in Howard Spring's *Fame Is the Spur* is thought to be Ramsay MacDonald. The governor-dictators who rampage through Dos Passos' *Number One*, Adria Langley's *A Lion Is in the Streets*, and Robert Penn Warren's *All the King's Men* look and act much like Huey Long. The novelist ranges backward into time as does the scientist. Maugham's *Then and Now* brings to life the wily Niccolo Machiavelli, and Samuel Shellabarger's *Prince of Foxes* reexamines the sinister Cesare Borgia. When the novelist goes forward into time he need not be confined to a mathematical extrapolation of birth rates, trade balances, or electoral trends. Instead, he can create, whole and entire, the world which he thinks will grow out of the one in which he lives or which he sees emerging. The scientist may attempt to define the group mind or examine pressures toward enforced conformity in political thought. But George Orwell in *1984* creates his own terrifying vision of the world thirty years from now. And this story is frighteningly believable. It does not even require Coleridge's "willing suspension of disbelief which constitutes poetic faith." With its three superstates perpetually at war, its Newspeak vocabulary including "thoughtcrime" and "doublethink," its omnipresent Big Brother, *1984* reflects aspects of our world out of which the novelist's vision grew. Besides the political apparatus which Orwell builds, he creates a protagonist, Winston Smith, one man out of all the masses of Party members and Proles who revolts against the system, providing the reader with a focus for personal association. The reader follows him through his round of duties in the Ministry of Truth, into his state-forbidden love affair, and finally down into the depths of the Ministry of Love where he is tortured into conformity before he will be "vaporized" and poured into the stratosphere as gas. If he likes, the author can move at will seven centuries into the future, where Aldous Huxley erected his *Brave New World*. From a world of mechanization, deteriorating family ties, and ascendant pragmatic science, he can artistically extrapolate a planet ruled cooperatively by ten World Controllers. Embryos are conditioned within their glass flasks and then decanted into a rigidly stratified society where stability has outlawed change and Ford has replaced God. And there are memorable people—sensuous Lenina Crowne, and the Savage, a "natural man" who commits suicide rather than choose between prehistoric primitivism and soulless modernism.

Not only does the novelist have complete freedom in time and space, he has the right to use any of the devices found attractive in communication since the first articulate primate squatting in the firelight gave his interpretation of experience to his hairy brothers. The point of the story can be driven home or made more palatable with laughter, suspense, or a cops-and-robbers chase that will make it memorable. Ernest Hemingway's Spanish guerrillas and Ignazio Silone's Italian peasants are often amusing. The reader may remember the inspired profanity or the droll proverbs; he will also remember the fight against Fascism and oppression. From *Darkness at Noon* the reader will take with him Rubashov's midnight arrest, the wait for the NKVD bullet in the back of the neck; he will retain, too, the irony of the disillusioned Bolshevik destroyed by the monster he helped create.

This attempt to differentiate the novelist's approach from the scientist's is not meant to prove that the novelist's is better. It is simply different, representing another aspect of the difference between science and art. Each discipline tries to describe and interpret experience. Where one does it by means of well-defined, rigidly controlled techniques within generally accepted boundaries, the other is highly flexible, embodying a view of life shaped by an individual set of preferences and dislikes, talents and blind spots. Each of these divergent methods offers advantages and disadvantages. One should not go to political novels expecting to find, except in rare cases, complete objectivity, solidly documented references, and exhaustive expositions of political theory. He should not always anticipate credibility. When problems are presented, the reader may not find answers or even indications of the directions in which they may be found. But one cannot go to a scientific monograph with the hope of meeting in its pages someone whose life is an embodiment of a problem, or whose survival represents the gaining of a goal, his death the losing of it.

These two approaches to the study of politics complement each other, just as the physician and clergyman both mean to keep their identical patient and parishioner well and whole. The novelist can, however, enter well into the scientist's field. When he deals with actual events, he tries to record them as they happened. If the names and places are changed, he is usually faithful to the manner or meaning of the events. In *Bricks Without Straw* Albion W. Tourgée assures the reader that these events or others exactly like them took place during the Reconstruction era in the South, and there is no reason to doubt him. Sinclair's *Oil!* exhaustively treats the Sacco-Vanzetti case; it is completely opinionated, but it is a historical account, nonetheless, of one of the most memorable political cases in American history. More than a historian, the political novelist is also an analyst. He sees cause-effect relationships at work, he looks into stimulus and response, motivation and satisfaction. Stendhal is not content merely to describe military and political events during the Napoleonic era; he goes beneath the surface to explain what some of them meant.

The Purposes of This Study

This examination of the political novel will go beyond simply charting its development. In order to examine it as a distinct literary form, it will be necessary to discuss its practitioners, the literary techniques they use, the purposes they aim at, and their success in achieving them. More than this, there will be attention to the function of these political novels, at the time they were written and now in our time. In the forefront will be an attempt to show what the reader can learn, whether he approaches this body of work from a particular discipline such as political science or literature, or whether he goes to it as a general reader wanting either enlightenment or entertainment.

The purposes and scope of each chapter indicate the purposes of the study as a whole. Chapter Two, "The Novel as Political Instrument," examines the effect of the political novel on politics. Some novels contain heroes presented against a political background which might just as well have been mercantile or medical; other novels are intended to have politics as their subject; still other novels are meant to have definite political consequences. This chapter is chiefly concerned with novels of this last type. But it is necessary to look at others, too, for in creating life in his novel the artist will often reflect his own preferences, and they may affect those of his reader. Chapter Three, "The Novelist as Political Historian," describes the way in which the writer may weave into his story the threads of history, recording not only the lives of his creations, but actual events in the lives of nations. By virtue of his special skills, he can recreate these events with a vividness found in few scholarly histories. Chapter Four, "The Novel as Mirror of National Character," is devoted to an examination of the cultural and national differences discernible in these novels. There appear to be some denominators of political behavior which remain common no matter what the scene of action. This chapter deals with the numerators, the quantities which vary from culture to culture. Chapter Five, "The Novelist as Analyst of Group Political Behavior," demonstrates the insight the novel can give into political actions which derive from group attitudes, pressures, and responses rather than individual ones. The novelist may use several indices to determine how a society is structured, which of its groups is most homogeneous, which most apparent in the effect it has upon the body politic. Chapter Six, "The Novelist as Analyst of Individual Political Behavior," shows how the basic unit in all political equations is treated. The novelist portrays the person who moves in the main stream of politics and the one who stands on its edges. In most cases the acts of these people are examined—their motives, their effects. As in any other kind of fiction, characters are created who are complete individuals, believable and unique. But sometimes they are also typical of a number of people. Chapter Seven, "Some Conclusions," emphasizes the major points made in the study. It also discusses what may be expected of the political novel in the future. The annotated bibliography gives the author, title, and date for each novel.

In terms of organization, this study proceeds from the most direct relationship between the novel and politics to the least direct relationship. Chapter Two shows how this art form can actually influence the political process. Chapter Six, on the other hand, indicates the way in which the novel treats the individual, who, with the exception of the outstanding leader, has far less direct influence upon politics than groups or nations. Chapter Three deals with the way in which the novel has recorded some major events in the political scientist's field from the early nineteenth century to the present. Chapters Four through Six proceed from larger to smaller political units.

In short, the aims of this study are to indicate the gradual development of the political novel in England and the United States, to show what it has produced in several other countries, and to demonstrate the insights it can give in this area of human behavior to students of literature, politics, and related disciplines, and to the general reader.

chapter two

The Novel as Political Instrument

A political novel written from a point of view favoring a particular faction is a political instrument in effect even if not in intent. A writer may sternly tell himself at the outset that he will be completely impartial, only to have the reviewers note all sorts of bias, real or imagined, of which he may not have been conscious. This happened to Turgenev when he published *Fathers and Sons*, and it continues to happen every year. The intensity of the authors' feelings varies from obsessive preoccupation to passing interest. The novels in this chapter were included because they contain definite opinions, sometimes appeals, on political subjects. Some of them never exhort the reader or seem to lead him by the hand to the author's point of view. But each of them contains material capable of influencing the reader's opinions about some phase of political activity. If a novelist gains a reader's support for a cause, arouses his distaste for a course of action, or simply produces a reevaluation of previously accepted beliefs, his work has served as a political instrument just as surely as a pamphlet mailed by a national committee or a handbill stuffed into the mailboxes of a sleeping city.

THE UNITED STATES

Harriet Beecher Stowe and the Civil War

Uncle Tom's Cabin is a prime example of the novel as political instrument both in intent and effect. Harriet Beecher Stowe declared in her preface that

The object of these sketches is to awaken sympathy and feeling for the African race, as they exist among us; to show their wrongs and sorrows, under a system so necessarily cruel and unjust as to defeat and do away with the good effects of all that can be attempted for them . . .

The book did more than awaken sympathy; its millions of copies helped rouse the growing anti-slavery sentiment in the North, creating in part the political climate out of which the Civil War grew and mustering moral support for its prosecution. But the novel's effects were not confined to America. In *Literary History of the United States* Dixon Wecter called it "the most influential novel in all history," and Harold Blodgett noted that it was used in the campaign that secured England's Reform Act of 1867.

Raymond Weaver, in his introduction to the Modern Library edition, notes that half a million Englishwomen signed an address of thanks to the author, and that Russians were said to have emancipated their serfs after reading the book. The hero of Edgar Lee Masters' *Children of the Market Place* says the book "was not really true," but he records the praise it won from Macaulay, Longfellow, George Sand, and Heine, and adds, "The winds of destiny previously let loose were blowing madly now."

Translated into nineteen languages, the novel was also dramatized. Eliza's flight across the ice and Simon Legree's cruelty have become hackneyed, but the author did not rely exclusively on such melodrama and tugging at the heartstrings. The plot is interlarded with case histories of slavery—mothers whose children were taken from them, women sold for "breeders," men taken from their families and sent down into the deep South. The reader may feel that Legree is a villain so fiendish as to be unbelievable; he may find the angelic Little Eva's death scene, in which she cuts off golden curls and distributes them to the sobbing family and retainers, cloying or emetic. There are other characters, though, worth observing. Senator Bird of Ohio, who had formerly supported the Fugitive Slave Act, shelters Eliza before sending her to a Kentuckian who had freed his slaves and now runs a stop on the Underground Railway. Artistically the novel is very bad. Its structure sprawls, its melodrama creaks, and its sentiment oozes over hundreds of pages peopled more often by cardboard figures than believable human beings. This is another case, however, in which the reading public paid no attention to critical standards. Mrs. Stowe concluded her novel with the warning that

not surer is the eternal law by which the millstone sinks in the ocean, than that stronger law, by which injustice and cruelty shall bring on nations the wrath of Almighty God!

Her words were prophetic, and her book helped to bring about the *dies irae* of which she spoke.

Albion Tourgée: The Blunders of Reconstruction

Just as the political novel helped to prepare the way for the Civil War, so it commented upon the events which followed it. In *A Fool's Errand* (1879) and *Bricks Without Straw* (1880), two awkward but intensely felt books, Albion Tourgée criticized the tremendous blunders of the federal government in the Reconstruction era. Using the same techniques of case history, pathos, and melodrama as did Mrs. Stowe, Tourgée applauds the intent of the federal Reconstruction program but is outraged and cynical at the way it was carried out. He praises the work of the Freedmen's Bureau but laments its dissolution and the government's virtual abandonment of the Negro. Like Mrs. Stowe, Tourgée states the problem as dramatically and appealingly as he can; then he offers his solution: education. Both of Tourgée's novels close with appeals for federal aid to education in the South. The Negro is obviously in greatest need, but the aid is meant to be spread over the entire educational system. Discarding all pretense at fiction and writing directly to the reader, Tourgée concludes *A Fool's Errand* by telling him that "Poor-Whites, Freedmen, Ku-Klux and Bulldozers are all alike the harvest of ignorance. The Nation can not afford to grow such a crop."

Perennial Theme: Corruption

In the 1880s the American political novel began to shift from the Civil War and Reconstruction to the theme of corruption. This subject was explored extensively during the next five decades. Whether the scene was the national capitol, as in Henry Adams' *Democracy* (1880), or a ward in New York City, as in James L. Ford's *Hot Corn Ike* (1923), the theme was the same—the betrayal of public trust for private ends. Although many of these novels were written in the resurgent school of Realism, all of them, in their depiction of pervasive corruption, were capable of being political instruments through the nature of the material which they treated if not through their author's intent. Whether the writer declaims through his hero against public robbery or simply tries to present dispassionately what he sees, the revulsion of the reader at the travesty of American political ideals is likely to be the same.

There was one notable exception to this trend. It was Jack London's *The Iron Heel* (1908). Projecting his story into the future, he wrote of an America under the dictatorship of an Oligarchy serving the interests of the large corporate and industrial groups. The reader learns that the Oligarchy was eventually overthrown, but the book concentrates upon a fictitious era of horrors unequalled until the appearance of Orwell's *1984* forty years later. In his introduction to the novel, Anatole France called London a Revolutionary Socialist. This he was, and—in the novel, at least—a devoted Marxist as well. The book was clearly meant to be a political instrument. Its fulfillment of this aim may be judged by a comment of Stephen Spender in his contribution to *The God That Failed* (1950). He remarks that Harry Pollitt, a high official of the English Communist Party, had told him that in his opinion *The Iron Heel* was "the best revolutionary novel." The Communist view of the propaganda value of literature makes the comment significant.

Upton Sinclair: Corruption Plus Radicalism   Upton Sinclair's books were among those which marked the beginning of a transitional phase in the American political novel. In them a new theme was added to that of political corruption: the rise of leftist and radical forces. *Oil!* (1926) focuses on Bunny Ross's political journey to the far Left. Bunny's father, J. Arnold Ross, is one of the tycoons who selects, pays for, and elects an American president. Naming names and placing places, Sinclair sends his characters into the campaign of 1920. Verne Roscoe says that he is negotiating with Barney Brockway of "the Ohio gang." Sinclair writes that "he made exactly the right offers, and paid his certified checks to exactly the right men," and Warren Harding was nominated. The fifty million dollars poured into the campaign by the oil interests (according to Sinclair) helped to finish the job. The account of the naval reserve oil lease scandals which follows makes Sinclair's position on the activities of a powerful lobby very clear. More an exposé than a work of art, the novel describes attempts to hinder the organization of the oil workers and the strikes and strike-breaking which follow. The book ends with an attack upon

an evil power which roams the earth, crippling the bodies of men and women, and luring the nations to destruction by visions of unearned wealth, and the opportunity to enslave and exploit labor.

Two years later Sinclair threw himself into a vindication of the characters and lives of Nicola Sacco and Bartolomeo Vanzetti. The cast of *Boston* (1928) includes the fictitious Thornewell family, but they are all dwarfed by the two Italians whose careers ended in the electric chair. Sinclair presents the case as an effort by the city and state governments to dispose of two representatives of the anarchist movement which was thought to threaten society's foundations. He maintains that the government was supported in its attempt by representatives of organized religion as well as the socially prominent and economically powerful classes. Although the author said that he had tried to be a historian, that he had not "written a brief for the Sacco-Vanzetti defense," the novel is precisely that. It is also an indictment of most of the immediate society in which the events took place. He accuses the prosecution of carefully building an illegal, trumped-up case heard by the violently prejudiced Judge Thayer. He declares that the Commission which investigated the case, made up of Cardinal O'Connell, Bishop Lawrence, and President Lowell of Harvard, rendered an endorsement of the state's actions which amounted to a whitewash. Running parallel to the story of the Italians is that of Jerry Walker, parvenu tycoon of the New England felt industry who is legally plundered by the old commercial and banking interests of Boston and New York. Mr. Sinclair's intentions to be impartial may have been sincere, but like the exclamation points in his prose, they got away from him.

Growing Political Consciousness: 1930 to 1954

The great wave of political consciousness which struck America in the 1930s surged over into the novel. It took several forms. There was the novel which advocated liberal reforms in government, and the novel which, presenting the Communist point of view, necessarily went farther. The proletarian novel emerged. Sympathetically describing the privations of the so-called proletariat to stimulate betterment of its living conditions, these novels sometimes cleaved to the Communist Party line but were often the work of non-Communist authors writing from genuine concern for their subjects. The Communists regarded this art form as another weapon in the class struggle. Paul Drummond, a fanatical Communist writer in James T.

Farrell's *Yet Other Waters* (1952), shouts that "now the time has come for Party literature." Moses Kallisch, leader of a front organization starting a Left Wing Book Club, declares, "The day is not far off when we'll overwhelm bourgeois culture in America!" Increasing consciousness of the political malignancy of Fascism and Nazism appeared in the novel. With the descriptions of these dangers came appeals for the strengthening and defense of the best in the American political system.

John Steinbeck: The Party Organizer   Appearing in 1936, Steinbeck's *In Dubious Battle* sociologically described the violent course and tragic end of a Communist-organized strike of apple pickers in California's Torgas Valley. Shortly after he applies for membership in the Party, young Jim Nolan is taken down into the valley by McLoed, a hard-shelled, veteran Communist organizer. The underpaid pickers, living in squalor, follow Mac when he helps precipitate the strike. As the apprentice, Jim follows each move carefully, learning both theory and practice from Mac, who wants violence and a prolonged strike in order to gain wide attention and pave the way for organizing subsequent picking operations. Adept and devoted, Jim learns quickly despite a gunshot wound and increasing hunger. He even assumes temporary leadership over Mac when the latter's vitality momentarily sags. At the book's end, with the strike failing, Jim falls into a trap and his face is blown off by a shotgun blast. Mac carries his body to the strikers' camp platform. The book's last line is Mac's funeral oration for Jim: "Comrades! He didn't want nothing for himself—" The novel may be considered a social and political study; the picture that emerges is one of economic oppression, embattled workers, and hard but devoted organizers.

Sinclair Lewis: Native Fascism   Sinclair Lewis's fifteenth book also appeared in 1936, and its title is an indication of the jolt it was meant to give to American complacency. *It Can't Happen Here* is the story of the American republic transformed into a Fascist corporate state through a military coup d'état made possible by an electorate which was attracted by share-the-wealth schemes, anti-minority agitation, and primitive emotionalism. The methods of the Nazis and Fascists are applied to eradicate the democratic system and even the boundaries of states. The country is divided into eight provinces, concentration camps devour the dissenters and the suspect, and all of American life is harshly regimented. Lewis's hero is "bourgeois intellectual" Doremus Jessup. After he has lost his newspaper, his daughter, and his son-in-law, he becomes a member of the New Underground. When revolution wins back only half the country, he enters the other half as a secret agent. This novel has most of the faults and virtues of Lewis's other books: character merging into caricature, complete lack of subtlety, and embarrassingly awkward dialogue; but with this there is accurate social criticism, a genuine if crude vitality, and—particularly in this novel—a very earnest concern for American traditions. Lewis's point is made clear as Jessup reflects that the tyranny of the dictatorship isn't primarily the fault of Big Business, nor of the demagogues who do their dirty work. It's the fault of Doremus Jessup! Of all the conscientious, respectable, lazy-minded Doremus Jessups who have let the demagogue wriggle in, without fierce enough protest.

John Dos Passos and Ernest Hemingway: Liberal Causes Abroad Glenn Spotswood's geographical and political odyssey, abruptly ended by a rebel bullet in the Spanish Civil War, forms the central theme of Dos Passos' *Adventures of a Young Man* (1938). Politically conscious even as a boy, Glenn becomes successively a transient worker, a *cum laude* college graduate, a Communist labor organizer, and a disillusioned member of a splinter group. Clearly and dispassionately, Dos Passos allows his story to unfold. There are unsavory, dislikable characters such as fierce but noncombatant Comrade Irving Silverstone and sinister Jed Farrington, an American Communist who, as a Spanish loyalist colonel, divides his lethal attentions between the rebels and political unreliables. But one has the feeling that the author is not leaning in any direction. In the prose poems interspersed throughout the novel, however, Dos Passos lectures his reader. The concluding paragraph analyzes the growth of the American Communist Party and explains the gullibility of the Americans deceived by it. The last lines tell the reader that

only a people suspicious of selfserving exhortations willing to risk decisions, each man making his own, dare call themselves free, and that when we say the people . . . we mean every suffering citizen, and more particularly you and me.

A little less obvious was the position of Ernest Hemingway in his fine novel *For Whom the Bell Tolls* (1943). Hemingway would very probably disclaim any intent to write a political novel, but his book teaches a lesson in one of the oldest and surest ways—by example. Robert Jordan has left his instructorship in Spanish at the University of Montana to go to Spain as a demolition expert for the loyalists. Although he has placed himself under Communist discipline for military reasons, he is not a Communist. He is a teacher who has taken a most un-sabbatical leave to fight Fascism in a country he loves. Following the pattern of most of these books, Hemingway sums up a few pages from the end. Badly injured and unable to make his escape, Jordan lies waiting in the forest to fight a fatal rearguard action which will buy time for his escaping friends. He thinks:

I have fought for what I believed in for a year now. If we win here we will win everywhere. The world is a fine place and worth the fighting and I hate very much to leave it.

In *Number One* (1943), Dos Passos shifted from dictatorship abroad to dictatorship at home. Chuck Crawford is reminiscent of the late Huey Long of Louisiana. Magnetic, dynamic, and unscrupulous, Chuck wins the governorship and then goes on to the United States Senate. His personal aide is the alcoholic Tyler Spotswood, Glenn's older brother. Served up as the goat in an oil lease scandal which breaks about Chuck's head, Tyler allows himself to remain silent and be convicted. This is primarily because of Glenn's last letter from Spain exhorting Tyler not to let them "sell out" the people at home. Tyler apparently feels that his conviction is an atonement for failure to accept the responsibility which Sinclair Lewis also said devolved upon each citizen. In the novel's last three lines Dos Passos looks the reader squarely in the eye: "weak as the weakest, strong as the strongest, the people are the republic, the people are you."

The Grand Design appeared in 1949 to complete the *District of Columbia* trilogy. In this third novel, Dos Passos' style remains the same—detached and impersonal, straightforward and clear. His politics (in the prose poems) seem unchanged. He appears to be liberal, to retain his sympathy for the smaller people having a difficult time economically. Since the book covers the war years, the danger represented by the Axis powers is evident, but the equally pernicious influence of militant international Communism is equally clear. Although the book is jammed with characters from many political strata, its primary focus is the career of Millard Carroll, who leaves his Texarcola business to join the New Deal Farm Economy Administration. As the war progresses, Carroll comes to feel that the Four Freedoms are being forgotten in its prosecution. He sees personal jealousies and conflicts within the administration. By implication, the program which produced relocation camps for Japanese-Americans helps to complete his disillusionment. Finally, crushed by personal tragedy, he resigns. The last line of the last prose poem tells the reader, "Today we must learn to found again in freedom our republic."

George Weller: International Communism In 1949 George Weller's *The Crack in the Column* drew attention to one of the widespread areas in which the Comintern was trying to extend Russian domination. The scene is Greece. The novel reaches its climax when ELAS, the army of the Communist-dominated EAM popular front group, fights the British in the streets of Athens while the American army contains the Germans' last great effort in the Ardennes. Shot down earlier on a mission, American bomber pilot Tommy McPhail decides not to be evacuated by the underground net of British Major Walker. He remains to engage in similar behind-the-lines work. Walker becomes McPhail's tutor in global politics as well as espionage. His primary subject is the need for the United States to accept responsibility for creating international conditions favorable to the West, as he says Britain has done. Walker tells McPhail that the United States must learn to recognize Soviet strategy and combat it by such means as permanent American bases in the Middle East. Once again, the most explicit statement of the book's message is saved for the end:

> You Americans just pay your way out of the positions of the last war, then [help] your way back into the same positions in the next. You forget that war is continuous and this everlasting series of visits to the strategic pawnshop a wasteful streak of postponement of the eventual showdown.

Like many other novels which can be regarded accurately as political instruments, this one, with its accomplished delineation of a complex situation, tangled relationships, and deep cross-currents, contains no direct appeals to the reader. Neither does it have any scowling villains or radiant heroes. But the portrayal of the growing political maturity of the naïve American under the tutelage of the able but weary Englishman may perhaps achieve the same effect, and do it better.

Norman Mailer: The Extreme Left   The voice of the extreme Left, rarely heard in recent American novels, sounded in Norman Mailer's *Barbary Shore*, a murky mixture of obscure symbolism, endless conversation, and political theory disguised as dialogue. Published in 1951, the novel met with a generally unfavorable critical reception. A reading bears out this verdict. McLoed, apparently speaking for the author as his *raisonneur*, discusses what he calls revolutionary socialism at great length. Rejecting Russian Communism as state capitalism, McLoed's two-thousand-word, non-stop lecture envisions a mutually destructive war between "the Colossi." The Lenin of tomorrow, with the surviving theorists and proletariat, must be ready to spring to the barricades of the rubble-strewn "hundred Lilliputs" which survive. Before he is killed, McLoed passes his concept of Marxian revolutionary socialism like a Grail or a sword to Mikey Lovett. He is to keep it in readiness for the day when it can be used. This novel is intensely political. Despite its ambiguousness and withheld secrets, its essential point emerges: the first socialist revolution was betrayed; the true revolutionary socialism must make the second one successful.

Novels of the Cold War   As wartime cooperation with the Russians was superseded by a growing awareness of the nature of militant Communism and the Moscow-oriented loyalties of American Communists, the novel chronicled this awakening. In *The Grand Design* Paul Graves had told Millard Carroll that a Russian purchasing commission or a Russian-controlled political party meant "espionage and counterespionage and counter-counterespionage ad infinitum . . ." Novels like Irwin Shaw's *The Troubled Air* (1951) and William Shirer's *Stranger Come Home* (1954) recorded the violence of this reaction. The function of these novels as political instruments was to rouse indignation against the forces which, in seeking to destroy American Communism, use methods as authoritarian and undemocratic as those of the Soviets themselves. Both novels enlist the reader's sympathies on the side of loyal, non-Communist Americans who are unjustly attacked by self-appointed judges using lies and questionable methods. These courageous protagonists are virtually ruined professionally and economically, for their integrity forbids them salvation through conformity forced upon them by fanatical groups. *The Troubled Air* embodies the problem in the efforts of director Clement Archer to keep his radio actors employed until they can defend themselves against charges of Communism made by *Blueprint*. This magazine, like some which have appeared on the American scene, specializes in allegations of Communist Party membership or sympathies on the part of entertainers. Archer's actions, exceedingly dangerous to his own position through his lack of awareness of the nature of his opponents, cost him his job. This novel is less a *roman à clef*, more complex, and far more accomplished than Shirer's book. Archer is victimized not only by *Blueprint* and the people who sur-render to it, but by two of the people he defends. Frances Motherwell renounces Communism and denounces Archer. Vic Herres, an old friend and secretly a fanatical Communist, has acted for his cell in selecting Archer as a "convenient point of attack," one who would fight the Com-munists' battle for them. The novel thus records the painful education of an honorable man whose naïveté about American Communists is matched by his ignorance of their opponents who borrow Communist methods. The book is very well done, and in the reader-association with Archer which it produces, it provides a vicarious ordeal of arbitrarily assumed guilt-by-association with no recourse to conventional legal relief.

Stranger Come Home is a fictionalized account of a group of similar cases familiar to most newspaper readers. Here the spark is ignited by a publication called *Red Airwaves*. Commentator Raymond Whitehead has been blacklisted after his defense of Foreign Service officer Stephen Burnett, accused of Communist sympathies before the investigating committee of Senator O'Brien. Burnett is charged with conspiring to give China to the Communists. He has actually done nothing more than follow the foreign policy of the Roosevelt and Truman administrations and criticize the corruption he saw in the regime of Chiang Kai-shek. Whitehead succes-sively loses his sponsor, his air time, and his job. While he is in Europe he is accused by Senator O'Brien of being a Soviet agent. This charge is based upon the testimony of two ex-Communists who have become pro-fessional witnesses against people like Burnett and Whitehead. To give immediacy and the personal impact of the experience, the book is written in diary form. Although its fidelity to actual events makes it seem a transcription and though its quality as a work of art is not outstanding, the novel succeeds in driving its point home. The villains are quite black and the heroes are quite white despite the peccadillo here and there meant ap-parently to humanize them. Nevertheless, the reader who grants belief and sympathy to Burnett and Whitehead will be hard put to suppress indigna-tion and fear at the people, methods, and events which combine to bring near ruin to two intelligent and patriotic United States citizens.

In 1952 Paul Gallico's *Trial by Terror* chronicled the ordeal of Jimmy Race, reporter for the Paris edition of the *Chicago Sentinel*. Slipping into Hungary to unearth the story behind the conviction and twenty-year sentence meted out to an American named Frobisher, Race is arrested. Brainwashed and tortured into a false confession at a propaganda trial, Race is sentenced to prison. When his release is eventually secured, he is a fear-ridden, completely disorganized personality, an animal conditioned to confession as completely as Pavlov's dog was to salivation. But his destruction is not the only cause for anger. His liberation was not achieved by his government, but by his editor, who was able to blackmail the

Hungarian Minister of Affairs because of Titoist activities. The feeling throughout the book is that the United States embassy played a diplomatic game in which the deadliest weapons were strongly worded notes. The final irony is that the release was accomplished by a private citizen forced to use Communist methods of blackmail and intimidation. This novel graphically indicts Soviet brutality. It also criticizes American policy in a dramatic aspect of the cold war.

GREAT BRITAIN

The English political novel appeared somewhat earlier than its American counterpart. Its subjects range over a wider area and its varieties of political experience are more numerous. As a political instrument, however, the English novel is very like the American.

Benjamin Disraeli: Revitalized Toryism

In the preface to the fifth edition of *Coningsby*, coming five years after first publication in 1844, Benjamin Disraeli, later Prime Minister and Earl of Beaconsfield, made no pretense about his intent:

The main purpose of its writer was to vindicate the just claims of the Tory party to be the popular political confederation of the country. . . . It was not originally the intention of the writer to adopt the form of fiction as the instrument to scatter his suggestions, but, after reflection, he resolved to avail himself of a method which, in the temper of the times, offered the best chance of influencing opinion.

This novel was the first of three which comprised Disraeli's *Young England* trilogy. In a somewhat unsubstantial way, the three books set forth the principles which were to create a revitalized Tory party. In *The Political Novel* Morris Speare concludes that the four major points of the program deal with the nobility, the middle class, the working class, and the English church. The nobility was to reassume the leadership it held before patents of nobility were doled out freely to clever entrepreneurs and favorite retainers of great families. An aristocracy in function as well as name, it was to be assisted by the vigorous industrial and mercantile middle class which had arisen in England since the industrial revolution. The lot of the working class was to be bettered by a sympathetic government rather than by militant movements from within its own ranks. Moral and spiritual leadership was to be supplied by a revitalized church true to its fundamental religious tradition. Harry Coningsby, grandson of the dissolute and immensely powerful Lord Monmouth, is the personification of Young England. A hero at Eton and Cambridge, he returns from a year of travel on the continent to enter politics. Refusing to sit in Parliament for one of Monmouth's rotten boroughs and act as a rubber stamp for old Tory policies, Coningsby is cut out of Monmouth's will. Monmouth's death and a neatly juggled legacy eventually pave the way for Coningsby's entry into Parliament on his own terms. Patly, Coningsby of the nobility marries Edith Millbank, daughter of a middle class tycoon.

A year later, *Sybil* followed *Coningsby*. Like substitutes in a football game, Charles Egremont and Trafford go in for Coningsby and Millbank. Much of the book is concerned with the working class. Disraeli shows the reader the horrible conditions in which many of its members live and the violence of their attempts to better them. Bishop Hatton, barbarous ruler of the locksmiths of the mining district village of Wodgate, leads his "Hell-cats" in an assault upon ancient Mowbray Castle. Unions are presented as groups of violent men, cloaked and hooded. Supplementing this portrayal is one of a decaying and greedy aristocracy. One can perhaps imagine the reaction of the landed or moneyed English voter. He might well accept Disraeli's opinion that something had to be done.

Tancred completed the trilogy in 1847. The hero is the sheltered great-grandson of the Duke of Bellamont, who "might almost be placed at the head of the English nobility." The introspective Tancred is preoccupied with religion and the direction it can give to human affairs particularly in the areas of politics and government. Unable to find the answers to his questions in England and unwilling to enter Commons until he has them, he makes a pilgrimage to the Holy Land. At this point the novel dissolves into a panorama of kidnapings, desert intrigues, and mountain kingdoms reminiscent of Rudolph Valentino movies. Tancred becomes absorbed with "the great Asian mystery" which is to assist in the moral regeneration of the West, particularly England. Overwhelmed by Emirs and Sheikhs, Turks and Druses, the novel is the weakest of the three. But together the books are a prime example of an art form carefully selected and used to gain a hearing for a political program.

Henry James: The Breakup of Victorian Tranquillity

The Princess Casamassima, published by Henry James in 1886, is one of the novels which focused upon the revolutionary currents beginning to stir beneath the surface of English political life. Irving Howe has called it a warning that something had to be done to alleviate the misery of the poor. These conditions had given rise to radical groups such as that which met at the Sun and Moon Tavern under the leadership of Paul Muniment. The personal tragedy of his friend Hyacinth Robinson forms the novel's central theme. The sensitive, disinherited inhabitant of two worlds, Robinson is the illegitimate son of a Frenchwoman who had murdered her titled lover. Robinson's maternal grandfather had fallen on the barricades of the French Revolution. Raised with the help of Eustache Poupin, exiled veteran of the French Commune, Robinson feels that he is heir to a revolutionary background. Emotionally exalted, he declares his willingness for self-sacrifice at a group meeting. From that time on, like the protagonist of *The Beast in the Jungle*, Robinson waits for the summons to fulfill his destiny. But meanwhile he falls under the spell of the Princess, who takes a dilettante interest in the lives of the poor and the activities of the radical movement. Partly under her influence and partly as a result of a trip to Venice and Paris made possible by a small legacy, Robinson finds his revolutionary ardor waning. In his admiration for the richness of European civilization, he becomes reluctant to act as an agent of its eventual destruction. When the summons comes for him to assassinate a duke, he shoots himself instead. James presents a gallery of types: the guilty aristocrat, a member of the decayed gentility, the professional revolutionary, and the industrious poor. In this novel James is concerned as always with personal relationships, backgrounds, and motivations. He also presents an environment out of which political violence can explode. And his feelings about the need for preventing it are clear.

Joseph Conrad: Early Cloak and Dagger

In 1907 Joseph Conrad explored this problem from the same point of view in *The Secret Agent*. In the author's note which introduced the novel, Conrad wrote that a friend had mentioned anarchist activities. This was the germ of the story:

I remember, however, remarking on the criminal futility of the whole thing, doctrine, action, mentality; and on the contemptible aspect of the half-crazy pose as of a brazen cheat exploiting the poignant miseries and passionate credulities of a mankind always so tragically eager for self-destruction. That was what made for me its philosophical pretences so unpardonable.

Conrad then had his point of view; his recollection of an attempt to blow up the Greenwich Observatory gave him the outlines of his plot. A "delegate of the Central Red Committee," Adolf Verloc is actually an informer and *agent provocateur* for many years in the pay of the embassy of a "great power" (probably Russia). His principal function is to transmit warnings of planned bomb-throwings to insure the safety of "royal, imperial, or grand-ducal journeys . . ." Called to the embassy, Verloc is told by first secretary Vladimir that the conference in Milan is lagging in its "deliberations upon international action for the suppression of political crime . . ." England is chiefly responsible, Vladimir tells him. He orders Verloc to provide a stimulus in the form of an attack "with all the shocking senselessness of gratuitous blasphemy." Verloc is ordered to blow up the Observatory. Always a businessman and never a terrorist, he is deeply disturbed. Obtaining a bomb, Verloc sends his admiring half-wit brother-in-law Stevie out with it. But Stevie stumbles and blows up himself rather than the Observatory. When Verloc's wife learns what has happened, she kills him and then commits suicide. To add to the impact of the story, Conrad wove into it the characters of Karl Yundt, an evil old terrorist, and the Professor, a "perfect anarchist" who spends his life in experiments to develop the perfect detonator. In *The Great Tradition* F. R. Leavis has rightly called this book "one of Conrad's two supreme masterpieces." In its structure, its delineation of personality, and its masterful manipulation of point of view, the book is a classic. It is an example of the superiority of the European political novel, one of the finest works in the entire genre.

Under Western Eyes was written from the same point of view as *The Secret Agent*. Appearing in 1910, the novel dealt with the same sort of groups Conrad had treated three years earlier. But now the area was wider, the figures larger, and the stakes bigger. Kirylo Razumov, another illegitimate like Hyacinth Robinson, is studying at St. Petersburg University for a career in the civil service. His life is disrupted when Victorovitch Haldin seeks refuge in his rooms after blowing up the President of a Repressive Commission which had imprisoned, exiled, or hanged many Russians considered disloyal to the Czar. Afraid of being suspected of complicity and enraged at what he feels is gratuitous destruction of the only life he can make for himself, Razumov, on the advice of his father, Prince K———, betrays Haldin to the police. His life now completely disoriented, Razumov is persuaded by the Prince and Councilor Mikulin to go to Geneva. Regarded as a hero and the accomplice of Haldin, he enters the revolutionary circle led by the famous Peter Ivanovitch. His job is to report their plans to Mikulin. But then, despite himself, he falls in love with Haldin's sister Nathalia. He confesses his betrayal of Haldin to her and then to the circle. Maimed by the circle's executioner, Razumov stumbles out onto the street and into the path of a tram car. At the novel's end he has returned to Russia with but a short time to live. Again, Conrad's point of view affects the reader through the tragedies he describes, the object-lesson characters he creates, and the comments they make. The narrator and Conrad's *raisonneur*, an anonymous teacher of English in Geneva, is the source of many of these comments. When he sees Nathalia about to return to Russia as a dedicated worker, he thinks of her believing in "the advent of loving accord springing like a heavenly flower from the soil of men's earth, soaked in blood, torn by struggles, watered with tears."

E. M. Forster: The Problem of Imperialism

Out of E. M. Forster's *A Passage to India* (1924) comes a compassionate plea for British understanding of India. But even understanding is not enough; there must also be love. This great subcontinent, divided by geography, economics, caste, and religion, has a heritage of misery and discord. The book's two great themes are the divisions which sunder India and the love which alone can make it whole. It has been taken by the British without love in a union which is rape. In one of the parallels which inform the theme, this action is represented on the interpersonal level by the projected loveless marriage of Adela Quested and British civil servant Ronny Heaslop. The novel moves to a climax when the hysterical Adela mistakenly accuses the sensitive Dr. Aziz, a Mohammedan Indian, of attempted rape in the sinister Marabar caves. Aziz is aquitted, but his career is ruined and his spirit desolated. But the influence of Ronny's dead mother, Mrs. Moore, returns, through the memory of her and the presence of her two other children, to dispel some of the evil. At the book's end Aziz achieves a partial reconciliation with Cyril Fielding, the Englishman who has defended him at the cost of ostracism. But as they part Aziz shouts:

If it's fifty-five hundred years we shall get rid of you, yes, we shall drive every blasted Englishman into the sea, and then . . . you and I shall be friends.

As an appeal either for love or withdrawal from India, the book is a political instrument. It is also a revealing commentary upon one of the causes of what Winston Churchill called "the dismemberment of the British Empire."

Aldous Huxley and George Orwell: The Future in Perspective

Huxley's *Brave New World* (1932) and Orwell's *1984*, which followed it seventeen years later, are political instruments through the horror and revulsion they will create in any reader whose political beliefs are formed by the democratic tradition. Although both these fine novels are written in the future, neither is a fairy tale spun from air. Their only resemblance to fairy tales is a horde of enough all-too-real goblins and witches to make a month of *Walpurgisnachts*. Huxley, using godlessness and immorality, and Orwell, using totalitarian government, create nightmares well calculated to increase resistance to tendencies in modern life which could produce the results so strikingly conjured up in their novels.

THE CONTINENT

Ivan Turgenev and Fyodor Dostoyevsky: Nihilism and Its Rejection

In his helpful introduction to the Modern Library edition of *Fathers and Sons*, Herbert Muller writes that Ivan Turgenev's *A Sportsman's Sketches*, which appeared in 1852, had created an effect similar to *Uncle Tom's Cabin* in America. *Fathers and Sons* (1862), treating revolutionaries like most of Turgenev's books, had an even more lasting effect. Although both the uproar and the Nihilist movement died down, Muller declares that the novel "helped to form the mentality of the later revolutionaries who established the Soviet Union." The story deals with the return from college of Arkady Kirsanov and his friend Yevgeny Bazarov. Nihilist Bazarov dominates his disciple Arkady. Conflict quickly erupts. Arkady's father Nikolai is hurt by the distance between them, and his uncle Pavel seizes upon a pretext for a duel in which Bazarov wounds him. Bazarov's father Vassily, pathetically eager to be close to his son, finds the gulf between them even greater than that separating Arkady and Nikolai. The two generations—one giving allegiance to religion and the old regime, the other to science and revolutionary Nihilism—have lost almost all rapport with each other. Turgenev treats the perennial aspect of this theme, yet he particularizes it to mid-nineteenth century Russia. Eventually the gap between the Kirsanovs is narrowed as Arkady marries and returns to administer the estate with his father. But before Bazarov leaves he lashes out at Arkady:

You're not made for our bitter, rough, lonely existence. . . . Our dust would get into your eyes . . . you're admiring yourselves unconsciously, you like to abuse yourselves; but we're sick of that—we want something else! we want to smash people!

It may be, as Muller says, that Turgenev's mind was with the sons and his heart with the fathers, that he tried to be fair. Here is a case in which, regardless of intent, a novelist helped to shape a movement which disrupted a world.

Tolstoy and Dostoyevsky reacted violently to Turgenev's work. The former challenged him to a duel and the latter attacked and caricatured him mercilessly as Karamazinov in *The Possessed* (1872), a violent attack upon Nihilism. In his introduction to the Modern Library edition, Avrahm Yarmolinsky declares that

Dostoyevsky's avowed intention in writing it was to drive home certain convictions of his, regardless of whether or not he met the requirements of the art of fiction. He wanted to deal a body blow to the rebels who threatened what he considered to be the foundations of Russian life. Originally he conceived his novel as a political lampoon, a pamphlet against the revolution.

In the massive book which he produced, Dostoyevsky fulfilled his purpose by showing the effect upon a provincial capital of a group of revolutionaries guided by a demoniac leader. Conspiracy, mob violence, arson, and murder temporarily disrupt government. Pyotr Verhovensky returns from revolutionary activity abroad to set up groups throughout Russia. He seeks to knit together this particular group by making all of them participate in the murder of a dissident member. Before he has fled and his group has been caught, three more people have been killed. Nikolay Stavrogin, the book's perverted central figure, is meant to be the messiah of Pyotr's movement. The ruin of the whole structure is complete when, on the last page, Nikolay dangles from his own silken noose. Recurring in the book and linked to its title is the image of the bibical Gadarene swine. Pyotr's father, estranged from his abusive son, is dying partly because of a chain of events set in motion by him. He asks that this passage be read to him and then exclaims:

Those devils that come out of the sick man and enter into the swine. They are all the sores, all the foul contagions, all the impurities, all the devils great and small that have multiplied in that great invalid, our beloved Russia, in the course of ages and ages.

The swine had plunged into the sea and destroyed themselves. Dostoyevsky wanted to insure that his countrymen would not, like lemmings, follow each other to destruction.

André Malraux: Pro-Communism

An index of changing times is the contrast between *The Possessed* and André Malraux's *Man's Fate*. This novel represented the opposite pole of political thought. Published in 1934, Malraux's book sympathetically followed the abortive Communist attempt to capture Shanghai in 1927. Under the leadership of half-French Kyo Gisors and others like him, the Chinese Communists wage a losing battle against the Kuomintang party of Chiang

Kai-shek. This time the gallery of revolutionary types—theorists, assassins, hard-core Party workers—is presented in a different light. They are heroes. The professional revolutionists and disinherited peasants are following a vision. Even when they receive the *coup de grâce* or await death in the boiler of a locomotive, eventual victory is seen transcending temporary defeat. Having given his cyanide to wounded comrades, the Russian Katov is still able to reflect as he awaits his horrible end that "he had fought for what in his time was charged with the deepest meaning and the greatest hope; he was dying among those with whom he had wanted to live; he was dying, like each of these men, because he had given a meaning to his life." These words are something like Robert Jordan's valedictory to life. But Jordan fought to preserve Spanish democracy and Katov died to establish Chinese Communism. The novel serves all causes.

Ignazio Silone: Disillusionment on the Left

The first of a remarkable group of modern political novels appeared in the same year as *Man's Fate*. It was Ignazio Silone's *Fontamara*. "The poorest and most backward village of Marsica," Fontamara is the scene of progressive encroachments of Fascism upon the life of its people. Exploited by The Promoter—a builder, banker, and local tycoon—the uneducated peasants successively lose most of their water supply, the profits from their hard-raised crops, and their right to talk about politics. When the protests of some of its people make it appear that Fontamara is resisting the Mussolini regime, Black Shirt thugs raid the village, abusing its people and wrecking houses. Goaded by the need for work, Berardo Viola and the son of the nameless narrator go to Rome to seek it. Fleeced of their money, they finally obtain the necessary certificates of moral character. But The Promoter has written upon them that the men are politically unreliable. Thrown into jail upon suspicion of distributing copies of *The Unknown Hand*, they meet the editor of this resistance leaflet. To save him, Berardo assumes responsibility for the paper and is beaten to death by the police. The editor succeeds in delivering a small press to Fontamara, where the villagers begin their secret paper, which they call *What Shall We Do?* This phrase is not only the title; it is printed at the end of each story of Fascist atrocity. At the book's end, the nameless narrator and his family are in hiding with Silone. The village has been wiped out by the Fascists. The book's last line—not in quotes and therefore Silone's question as well as the narrator's—is, of course, What Shall We Do?

Three years later, in 1937, the next of Silone's fine political novels was published. *Bread and Wine* marks the beginning of the disillusionment of Silone's heroes with Communism which culminates in *A Handful of Blackberries* (1953). Pietro Spina, the central figure of *Bread and Wine*, returns to Italy although hunted there as a Communist agitator. Ill and perplexed, he goes into hiding in the poor mountain village of Pietrasecca disguised as a priest, Don Paolo Spada. His disguise evolves into another self, reviving and intensifying the inner conflict he has always felt through a dual attraction to Christianity and Marxism. Before he returns to political action he achieves a sort of synthesis of what he thinks are the best elements of both beliefs, necessarily rejecting Russian Communism. Don Paolo tries to give his old teacher Don Benedetto the essence of his belief:

If a poor man, alone in his village, gets up at night and takes a piece of chalk or charcoal and writes on the village walls: "Down with the war! Long live the brotherhood of all peoples! Long live liberty!" behind that poor man there is the Lord.

In A Handful of Blackberries Rocco de Donatis returns to the village of San Luca at the end of World War II. Formerly a fanatical Communist, he breaks with the Party. The novel describes the Party's attempt to ruin his life and his fiancée's. Figuring in the story is an ancient trumpet traditionally used to call the peasants to action "when we just can't stand things any longer." Rocco's survival and the inability of the Communists to seize the symbolic trumpet to pervert it to their own uses signalize a sort of victory. In their total effect these novels are an indictment of both Fascism and Communism. Simply written yet powerful, they display a deep sympathy for the poor and oppressed.

Arthur Koestler: The Bolshevik on Trial

Like Orwell and Huxley, Arthur Koestler wrote a novel which, without one plea or exhortation, is a political instrument through the strong emotional and intellectual response which it can create. Darkness at Noon (1941) tells the story of Nicolas Rubashov, an old Bolshevik once second only to "No. 1" in what is unquestionably Russia. But now this legendary hero of the Revolution lies in a small isolation cell awaiting the ordeal which is to lead to confession and abnegation at a public treason trial. Through the use of flashbacks, this stark and powerful novel traces Rubashov's career. All the usual elements are there—the devotion to the Party, the cold betrayals, the blind obedience. Eventually the repressed questions had risen to the surface. In attempting to work them out Rubashov had arrived at disillusionment and "political divergencies." Eventually he concludes that the mistake was that "we are sailing without ethical ballast." The trial over, he is led down a dark corridor deep within the prison. He reflects that Moses was allowed to see the Promised Land. "He, Nicolas Salmanovitch Rubashov, had not been taken to the top of a mountain, and wherever his eye looked, he saw nothing but desert and the darkness of night." An instant later the bullet crashes into the back of his head. One is appalled not only at his career and those of the thousands of Rubashovs who have helped to create the Soviet state, but at the whole process which creates a Rubashov—and a No. 1.

AFRICA

The inclusion of novels on contemporary South Africa in this study comes near to disregarding the limits set up by our definition of the political novel, for certainly there is as much of the sociological and economic in these novels as there is in *The Jungle* or *The Grapes of Wrath.* They are included, however, because politics plays as vital a part in the South African problems portrayed in these novels as do the other two factors. While the Blacks in the Union of South Africa are not slaves, their treatment is an inflammatory subject, and the repressive measures taken against them are political by their very nature. The Nationalist Party of Prime Minister Malan owes its tenure in no small measure to its policy of *apartheid,* strict segregation of Blacks from Whites.

Alan Paton: The Race Question

One of the most eloquent opponents of *apartheid* is Alan Paton, a member of the Liberal Party and author of two fine novels dealing with the general problem of race relations in South Africa: *Cry, The Beloved Country* (1948) and *Too Late the Phalarope* (1953). Although both books focus primarily upon interpersonal relationships, the tragedies which they involve have their bases in the relations of the two races from which the interacting characters are drawn. *Cry, The Beloved Country* tells a moving and deeply pathetic story of the loss of two sons. The son of the Zulu Stephen Kumalo, an Episcopal clergyman, murders the son of James Jarvis, benefactor of old Kumalo's church. Ironically, in Arthur Jarvis Absalom Kumalo had killed a man who wanted to better the lot of Kumalo's people. In 1953 the equally moving *Too Late the Phalarope* set forth the tragic story of Pieter Van Vlaanderen, police lieutenant of Venterspan and hero to Black and White alike. Convicted of sexual relations with the unfortunate Negress Stephanie, he is sentenced to prison and disgrace under Act 5 of 1927, the Immorality Act. The immediate causes of Pieter's tragedy are his wife's inability to give him complete understanding and fulfillment, and the vindictive enemy he has created in Sergeant Steyn. But the underlying causes are those which infect the Union of South Africa with the virulent disease of racial hate and bigotry. Paton's books are not only compelling human documents, they are also pleas for the eradication of the disease.

One of the reasons for the novel's preeminence as the literary form superbly fitted to describe and interpret life is the space it gives the writer to erect his structure, to illumine the nature of an individual, to characterize a people, to describe both human units in relation to the world. With his thousands of words the novelist can impart the shape he wants to the elements which will make his own vision of life meaningful to his reader. There is no better example of this characteristic of the novel than these works which use its freedom to treat that increasingly complex phenomenon of human activity—politics in its broadest sense. And, assuming the artist's privilege, he often makes his work a personal thing, producing not only a work of art but a political instrument as well.

chapter three

The Novelist as Political Historian

If Art imitates Nature, the political novel imitates History. In almost all these novels the starting point is a series of actual happenings. Filtered through the artist's consciousness, they sometimes emerge in curious forms. But unless they are spun wholly from moonshine, like Crawford's *An American Politician*, they usually bear some clearly discernible relation to the events of real life. Here again, the variety is great. Koestler's *The Age of Longing* (1951) is set in Europe of the future. In his words, "it merely carries the present one step further in time—to the middle nineteen-fifties." An apprehensive continent, listening with one ear for the mushrooming of atomic bombs, anxiously watches the United States and Russia, feeling that its fate may be decided at any moment by a single move of either of the giants. Although the time is the future, the running account of these opponents' moves which accompanies the story is based upon Koestler's interpretation of recent patterns in international affairs. Perhaps he is too gloomy, but this is the pattern he sees: Russia trumpets alarms at what it claims is aggression of a "Rabbit State"; an international crisis occurs and the people clutch their Geiger counters and anti-radioactivity umbrellas; the crisis is averted and tension relaxes; the Rabbit State is absorbed by Russia as the United States sends a printed protest form. At the other end of the scale is the *roman à clef*, represented by novels such as Gallico's *Trial by Terror* and Shirer's *Stranger Come Home*, in which the characters seem to be fictional counterparts of real people. The conventional disclaimer, "any resemblance to actual people . . . ," is usually present, but the likeness is often too close to be explained by chance. A close parallel to the events in Gallico's book is provided by the experiences of Robert Voegler and William Oatis. The ordeals of these two Americans were not related, but to fictionalize and interconnect them is a logical procedure for the writer building his novel around the subject of Americans falsely arrested for espionage by Russian satellites.

The political novelist may cover a short period of time or he may widen his canvas to accommodate a whole era. Stendhal's *The Charterhouse of Parma*, covers three decades, beginning in 1796 with Napoleon's entry into Milan and ending years later in the post-Napoleonic period. Howard Spring's *Fame Is the Spur* extends from the hero's birth in 1865 to the day when, heavy with honors, he participates as a peer in the coronation of King George VI. And Hamer Shawcross is a politician, so the novel deals with three quarters of a century of Britain's political life. As selective as he wants to be, the novelist may comment upon any phase of political life. The subjects in these novels range from small-town corruption to international policy, from the rise and fall of men to the birth and death of parties.

Since the reader knows there is a good chance that he will get a deliberately subjective view of political history, there must be good reasons for spending time on novels rather than going directly to Commager, Beard, Macaulay, or Gibbon. Although a novelist may not make it as obvious as did Thackeray, he is a god whose characters are his creations. He looks into their minds and souls. He reveals their ambitions and exposes their doubts more completely than any historian can do, even equipped with the volumes of memoirs and apologias which appear periodically in literary rashes. Even if the writer does not deal with real people, as do Upton Sinclair and others, he may present a recognizable copy or a man so typical as to shed light upon a specific class of political beings. The historian may describe the Chartist riots or Borgia's capture of Sinigaglia, but he cannot do it with the vividness one finds in the accounts of Disraeli and Maugham. Only rarely does a book like *The French Revolution* appear, and writers like Carlyle are even more rare. Then too, if the novelist is perceptive and detached, his description and analysis may be as acute as that of the historian. Disraeli's known point of view may make the interpretation of history in *Sybil* suspect, but the aloofness and irony of Maugham's *Then and Now* not only add to a tale that is sometimes droll, they help to give keen portraits of two very considerable men—Cesare Borgia and Niccolo Machiavelli. The novelist has at his disposal all the resources of the historian, as witness Sinclair's use of the 3,900 pages of the Dedham trial testimony in the Sacco-Vanzetti case. But he can do more than research. He can follow his characters into Congress, into their offices, and into their beds. He can also enter into the secret places of the brain, where lie the ultimate springs of political action.

GREAT BRITAIN

The English political novels included in this study present a panorama of British history extending back to the early part of the nineteenth century. A reading of them creates a picture of gradual change, of a surprisingly orderly political evolution. Disraeli's novels portray an England of immense social and economic differences. Although patents of nobility are being granted with increasing frequency, the society is much more static than dynamic, with extremely little individual or group mobility. It is an England of rotten boroughs, of voteless millions. The country's political life goes on in accordance with carefully defined rules, and the players remain the same—the Whigs and Tories. The England of a hundred years later, seen in *Fame Is the Spur*, is a different land. The Monarchy and the Church, though changed, are still strong reference points in English life, but almost everything else has altered. The franchise is no longer the exclusive possession of the landed; suffrage has been extended to women. The old *laissez faire* economy has evolved into one with considerable state regulation. The Whigs have given way to the Liberals who, in turn, are about to be superseded by the Labour Party. Actually, a revolution has taken place, but it has occurred within the existing political framework.

George Eliot: The Early Nineteenth Century in the Midlands

George Eliot's *Felix Holt, the Radical* was published in 1866, but it dealt with English politics in 1832. The plot, with its double identities, confused litigation, and secret paternities, is labyrinthine. But the description of English elections is sharp and vivid. Both the Whig and Radical candidates hire mobs of miners and navvies to demonstrate for them. The result is a bloody riot quelled by troops. Harold Transome is a corrupt Radical; his foil is Holt, the honest Radical charged with a murder committed during the riot. The novel's ending may seem sentimental and contrived, but this does not lessen the value of the book as a study from which emerges the political complexion of Laomshire in the English midlands.

Benjamin Disraeli and Anthony Trollope: Whigs v. Tories

In his effort to point up the need for a Young England party, Disraeli exposes the abuses of early nineteenth century England. In *Coningsby* one sees the millionaire Monmouth manipulate the twelve votes he owns in Commons to attain a dukedom. In *Sybil* Charles Egremont attempts to fit himself for public life by first investigating the conditions of the working class. Thus Disraeli shows to his reader the farm and factory workers and the miners who signed the National Petition of the Chartists. He follows the House of Commons' rejection of the Petition and the great uprisings which follow. This author-politician does not simply offer his own partisan solution to his country's ills; he also shows the specific events and general climate which elicit it.

Disraeli and Trollope have been praised at each other's expense. Disraeli had immensely greater political experience, but Trollope was by far the better novelist. Trollope's books are much more readable, and the student of the political novel will find just as much information in them. Of his six parliamentary novels, three make particularly profitable reading. *Phineas Finn, The Irish Member* (1869) chronicles the rise and fall of a young Liberal. Standing in 186– for the Borough of Loughshane in County Clare, Finn comes in with the Liberal government which succeds that of the Tory Lord de Terrier. A member of the new cabinet is Mr. Gresham, obviously modeled after Gladstone. The leader of the Conservative opposition is Mr. Daubeny, who bears a striking resemblance to Disraeli. The Reform Bill for England carries and Finn becomes Under Secretary for the Colonies. When his conscience forbids him to conform to party policy by voting against the Reform Bill for Ireland, he resigns his office and returns to Ireland, feeling that he has ruined his career in any case. In *Phineas Redux* (1874) he returns to Parliament. Now Daubeny's Tories are in, hanging tenaciously to a dwindling advantage in order to retain patronage and power as long as possible. Daubeny's purposes are clear. Because of his parliamentary tactics, he earns from Trollope the sobriquets "the great Pyrotechnist" and "a political Cagliostro." The culmination of the novel's love story, with which Trollope parallels the politics, is a spectacular trial in which Finn is acquitted of murder. He is offered his old job at the Foreign Office, but once more he retires from the field. Finn reappears in *The Prime Minister* (1876). When Daubeny's government goes out, neither he nor Gresham can muster enough strength to form a new one. The result is that now familiar phenomenon, a coalition government. The new Prime Minister is the Duke of Omnium, and his Secretary for Ireland is Phineas Finn. The country prospers under the coalition. But eventually signs of strain appear, and with them the resignations of two ministers. Finally, in its fourth year, the coalition founders on the County Suffrage Bill. Winning his vote of confidence by the slim margin of nine, Omnium resigns. It is left for the next government to complete the near-assimilation of the county suffrages with those of the boroughs. The two thousand-odd pages of these novels contain close likenesses of real politicians. They also describe some of the basic issues and attitudes of this era, and detail the workings of three distinctly different types of ministries.

George Meredith: The Early Radical

In their *Outline-History of English Literature* Otis and Needleman describe Meredith's *Beauchamp's Career* as "a political novel suggested by the candidacy of Capt. Frederick Maxse of Southampton." Published in 1876 and spanning the years 1850–1862, the novel highlights Commander Nevil Beauchamp's return from distinguished service in the Crimean War to run for Parliament as a fire-eating Radical. With more descriptions of canvassing and elections, the novel also contains the frequently found criticism of the press, which is almost always regarded as an organ in which truth runs a very bad second to political expediency. Before the novel ends with Beauchamp's tragic drowning, Meredith has given the reader his record of another aspect of English political life on the local level in the mid-nineteenth century.

Mrs. Humphrey Ward: Victorian Portraits

One of the chief values of Mrs. Humphrey Ward's *Marcella* (1894) in the study of English political currents is its catalog of types. The novel follows the erratic romance of Marcella Boyce and Aldous Raeburn. Grandson of Lord Maxwell, an old Tory politician, Raeburn enjoys a successful career in Commons, eventually becoming an Under Secretary in the Home Office. But the obstacle to true love is politics. Aldous is a Tory, and Marcella is a Venturist, defined as "a Socialist minus cant." The love triangle is completely political, for Aldous' rival Harry Wharton sits as a

Liberal. He is, however, gradually drawing closer to the rising labor movement. At one point Wharton gives the complete Socialist program for the country districts. After a transitional period, he says, land and capital will be controlled by the state. The emancipation of the laborer will mean that "the disappearance of squire, State parson, and plutocrat leaves him master in his own house, the slave of no man, the equal of all." Wharton presides at the Birmingham Labour Conference, speaking for graduated income tax and nationalization of the land. At this conference Mrs. Ward introduces the reader to the leaders of this new movement, from the moderates to the violent radicals. In a concession to the happy ending, the author has Wharton discredited for a rascal, thereafter reuniting Marcella and Aldous.

H. G. Wells: England in Transition

In *The New Machiavelli* (1910) H. G. Wells dealt with Dick Remington, whose career is ruined like that of Parnell by an extra-marital affair. Before his fall, Dick changes from a Liberal to a Conservative. Reminiscent of Disraeli's novels (which he has read), he becomes a Young Imperialist of the New Tory movement. Dick's shifting of political allegiance is not at all uncommon. This change of loyalties appears much more often in the English novel than the American, and there is no opprobrium attaching to it. Dick's career, in which he takes his stand on such timely subjects as woman suffrage, is the story of a journey from one political faith to another. Its background is the political milieu of late Victorian and Edwardian England.

Howard Spring: Labour and the Course of Empire

Spring's massive *Fame Is the Spur* (1940) records many of the major events in English national life in the seventy-five year period ending in 1940. But one of the primary formative influences in John Hamer Shawcross' life took place forty-six years before he was born. It was the Peterloo Massacre of 1819, in which the working people gathered in Manchester to hear Orator Hunt were attacked by dragoons. This story, related by Hamer's great uncle, first fires his imagination and then becomes part of his stock in trade. Entering politics as "Shawcross of Peterloo," he carries the sabre which the old man had wrenched from a dragoon. One of the founders of the Labour Party, Shawcross scorns the Fabians and writes popular books on politics. In London he sees Kier Hardy take his seat as one of Labour's first M.P.'s Later his marriage is disrupted when his wife estranges herself from him for his opposition to her suffragist campaigns. Spring records the turbulence of these efforts—the pickets outside Parliament, the violence, the hunger strikes, and the "Cat and Mouse Act" (a convicted suffragist was placed under police surveillance so that she could be returned to jail when she appeared to have recovered from the effects of a hunger strike). Although Shawcross' part in the World War I coalition government is considered by many a betrayal of Labour, he becomes Minister of Ways and Means when Labour comes in again in 1924. Having lost his chance to be Prime Minister, partly because of his stand in 1914, Shawcross in 1931 puts in motion the formation of the National Labour Party, intended as part of the coalition which is to be formed to take measures against the depression. This is thought to be his final betrayal of the Labour Party and cause. As a reward he is made Viscount Shawcross of Handforth in the same year. His forty-year political career is at an end.

Joyce Cary: The Edwardian Age and After

Tom Wilcher, in Joyce Cary's *To be a Pilgrim* (1942), is nearing the end of a life much involved with politics. In this acute, witty, and compassionate book, Cary follows Wilcher's attempt to keep a representative of the family in Tolbrook, its old home, and to inculcate into his niece and her little boy the religion which has been so vital a part of his own life. Through his recollections of his own experience and that of his brother Edward, Wilcher gives a vivid record of tense moments in England's political life. He recalls the stormy days when he and Edward were pro-Boer, and the more explosive times which followed:

There are no political battles nowadays to equal the bitterness and fury of those we fought between 1900 and 1914. It is a marvel to me that there was, after all, no revolution, no civil war, even in Ireland. For months in the years 1909 and 1910, during the last great battle with the Lords, any loud noise at night, a banging door, a roll of thunder, would bring me sitting upright in bed, with sweat on my forehead and the thought, 'The first bomb—it has come at last.'

Ten years later, in *Prisoner of Grace*, Cary built a novel around the career of another Labour politician, Chester Nimmo. He secures attention and injuries through his pro-Boer agitation. Shifting his attack from the government to the landlords, he finally wins a seat in Parliament in 1902, later becoming Under Secretary for Mines. He is so intensely political that when he tells his son fairy tales, the wolf in *Little Red Riding Hood* has "a face just like Joe Chamberlain." The narrator, Nimmo's unhappy wife Nina, reflects that:

I suppose nobody now can realize the effect of that "revolution" on even quite sensible men . . . But the truth is that it was a real revolution. Radical leaders like Lloyd George . . . really did mean to bring in a new kind of state, a "paternal state," that took responsibility for sickness and poverty.

Like Shawcross, Nimmo stays on in the coalition cabinet of 1914, hoping to become Prime Minister at the war's end. But he loses his seat in the general elections of 1922. At the book's end he is, like Shawcross, a lord, but one who looks wistfully from the sidelines upon the struggle in the political arena.

THE UNITED STATES

The American political novel does not record changes as broad as those seen in the English political novel. Some of the reasons for this variance are clear. In mid-nineteenth century America, as now, there was no titled aristocracy, no state church, no narrow and restricted suffrage. Also, there was no nearby source of revolutionary political thought and action such as that which troubled James and Conrad. What is perhaps disturbing, however, is the theme most often treated. If the subject most common in the English novel is political change or evolution ameliorating injustice, the one most common in the American political novel is corruption. Nearly half the American novels considered are written around that theme. They present a history of political misrule in which one group succeeds another. After the carpetbaggers, scalawags, and Ku-Kluxers have disappeared, the bosses who rule by mortgage holdings appear. They are succeeded by the railroad interests. Utilities groups exercise power and are followed by the oil interests. In the latest phase, corrupt political power is exercised by gangsters. Domestic politics are almost always the subject of books appearing before the 1930s. From this time on, however, the novel becomes increasingly concerned with foreign ideologies and the role of the United States in world affairs.

Edgar Lee Masters: Expansion and Conflict

Edgar Lee Masters' *Children of the Market Place* (1922) takes English-born James Miles from his immigration to America in 1833 to his dotage in 1900. Despite Miles's successive activities as farmer, broker, builder, and real estate operator, his chief function is to chronicle the career of Stephen A. Douglas. The description of Douglas' rise is paralleled by an account of the expansion of the United States. Historical personages pass across the stage—Jackson, Clay, Polk, Webster, Calhoun, and Lincoln. The great issues of the times, such as the tariff and the bank, the Oregon dispute and the annexation of Texas, contribute to the book's atmosphere. Miles even describes the February Revolution in France, and recounts its impact upon each European country. After describing the founding of the Republican Party, he gives his eyewitness account of the Lincoln-Douglas debates. The Civil War is about to set fire to the land, but the main narrative breaks off at this point. Masters attempted to liven the book by giving Miles an octoroon half-sister who causes him to commit murder and is herself the victim of rape and persecution. But the novel's chief value in a study of this genre is its attempt to delineate Douglas and his political philosophy against the background of formative periods in America's history. The literary debits include a pell-mell, unconvincing style loaded with rhetorical questions and overpowering statistics.

Albion Tourgée: Slavery and Emancipation

In *Uncle Tom's Cabin* Harriet Beecher Stowe gave a vivid picture of the Underground Railway through which slaves escaped to Canada. Among her characters were abolitionists who aided them and agents hired to recapture them. The historical aspects of slavery and emancipation were treated more fully, however, by Albion W. Tourgée. *A Fool's Errand* (1879) tells the story of a man with the improbable name of Comfort Servosse. A lawyer and ex-Union officer like Tourgée, he had moved to the South after the war, as did the author. Referred to by Tourgée as "The Fool," Servosse attempts the difficult task of integrating himself and his family into the life of a Southern community while supporting the rights of the Negroes. His experience, extending from 1866 until his death in the late seventies, is one of progressive disillusionment. Thorough analyses of events support the conclusions he draws. Early in the book one reads a detailed account of President Johnson's plan for Negro suffrage and also a statement of the supplementary Howard Amendment. Having discussed the role of the secret, pro-North "Union League" in the South during the war, Tourgée goes on to detail the rise of the Ku-Klux Klan. Later he analyzes the acts of amnesty passed by some Southern states to protect from prosecution members of secret organizations such as the Klan. By 1877 the South is in political control of its land again. Its policy of suppression has succeeded. This was the fault, Tourgée tells the reader, of stupid and foolish Federal policies:

> Reconstruction was never asserted as a *right*, at least not formally and authoritatively. Some did so affirm; but they were accounted visionaries. The act of reconstruction was *excused* as a necessary sequence of the failure of the attempted secession: it was never defended or promulgated as a *right of the nation*, even to secure *its own safety*.

In 1880 Tourgée published *Bricks Without Straw*, which spanned a short period before the war as well as that after it. The book follows the career of a Negro named Nimbus from chattel to landowner. But the novel is no more a dispenser of sweetness and light than was its predecessor. Nimbus is driven from his farm by the same forces which had made a Southern home untenable for Comfort Servosse. The romance between Northern Mollie Ainslie and Southern Hesden LeMoyne is redolent of tears, misunderstandings, and pining hearts finally united. In spite of its melodrama and other nineteenth-century trappings, the book is valuable. The purpose and function of the Freedmen's Bureau are examined as well as the Black Codes which counterbalanced it. Tourgée also discusses at length the township system installed in the South during the Reconstruction era and its gradual destruction by totalitarian appointee government on the county level. Near the novel's end the reader sees the pitiful plight of Nimbus' friends victimized by the Landlord and Tenant Act which strengthened the sharecropper system and reduced many Negroes to serfdom.

John W. De Forest: Post-War Corruption

In *Honest John Vane* (1875) and *Playing the Mischief* (1876) John W. De Forest built his stories around corruption in post-war Congress. John Vane goes to Washington with a reputation for honesty. When he succumbs to his wife's pressure for money to finance social climbing, he is more circumspect but just as greedy as his colleagues. His tempter and mentor is Darius Dorman, called by the author "Satan's messenger" and apparently actually meant to be one, complete with smoldering sparks and the smell of sulphur. He tells Vane not to

> go into the war memories and the nigger worshipping; all those sentimental dodges are played out. Go into finance. The great national questions to be attended to now are the questions of finance. Spread yourself on the tariff, the treasury, the ways and means, internal improvements, subsidy bills, and relief bills. Dive into those things, and stick there. It's the only way to cut a figure in politics and to make politics worth your while.

The main character in *Playing the Mischief* is Josephine Murray, a young widow who uses her attractiveness to secure passage of a bill which awards her $60,000 compensation for a barn burned in the War of 1812. In the process of dealing with lobbyists and corrupting Senators she loses the love of Edgar Bradford, a stalwart young Congressman who has tried to dissuade her from her scheme. Rising in the House, he denounces the lobbying and bribery he sees, declaring that "Congressional legislation will soon become a synonym for corruption, not only throughout this country, but throughout the world."

Hamlin Garland: Enter the Farmer

Set in Iowa in the 1870s, Hamlin Garland's *A Spoil of Office* (1897) deals with the role of farmers' organizations in politics. Bradley Talcott, silent and clumsy but obviously a dark horse who will pay off handsomely, enters politics because it attracts him and because he wants to better himself "for *her*," as Garland insists on referring to Ida Wilbur. Before they are married in a haze of romance and comradely devotion to the farmers' interests, they work with the Grange and the Farmers' Alliance. Free trade, national banks, and woman's suffrage are discussed frequently, as well as the depredations of corporations. A sentimental and somewhat superficial book which substitutes clichés and catch-phrases for exploration in depth of causes and effects, *A Spoil of Office* is valuable for its recital of the farmer's early role in politics—if one can bear the surfeit of bucolic virtues and inarticulate devotion to a fair and exalted lady.

Winston Churchill and David Phillips: Bosses and Lobbies

In his "Afterword" to *Coniston* (1906), Winston Churchill wrote that "many people of a certain New England state will recognize Jethro Bass." But he denied that his book was a biography and added that "Jethro Bass was typical of his Era, and it is of the era that this book attempts to treat." Beginning his story shortly after Andrew Jackson had entered the White House, Churchill traces Bass's subsequent control of Coniston, Truro County, and then of the entire state (probably New Hampshire). His original lever is a sheaf of mortgages. Through this power over his mortgagers, he places his men (also mortgage holders) in office and builds his machine. By 1866 Bass has gained control of the state, which he runs from his room in the Pelican Hotel in the capital. He has transferred his devotion from his dead sweetheart, Cynthia Ware, to her child, Cynthia

Wetherell. His chief source of income is the railroad lobby, which pays handsomely for the legislation it purchases through the state legislature from him.

When Cynthia leaves him on learning his political methods, the saddened Bass begins to let his power slip away. The industrial and railroad interests start to combine while the Harwich bank stands by with mortgage money to help destroy his control. But Bass returns to fight one more battle when magnate Isaac Worthington has Cynthia dismissed from her schoolteaching job and disinherits his son Bob for wanting to marry her. Mustering his power in the legislature and showering Worthington with adverse decisions from supreme court judges he has made, Bass blocks Worthington's railroad consolidation bill. After compelling him to consent to the marriage and write conciliatory letters to the lovers, Bass lets the bill go through.

In *Mr. Crewe's Career* (1908), set twenty years later, Churchill described the power shift Bass had foreseen. The legislature is now owned by Augustus Flint, Worthington's former "seneschal" who controls the Northeastern Railroad. His "captain-general" who rules from Bass's old room in the Pelican is railroad counsel Hilary Vane. The star-crossed lovers in this novel are Victoria Flint and Austen Vane. Austen fights the railroads despite his father and foresees the day when a new generation, willing to assume its political responsibilities, will turn out the railroad group. After a quarrel, Hilary leaves Flint but agrees to stay on for the gubernatorial nomination battle. As Flint watches Vane stalk from his study he sees "the end of an era of fraud, of self-deception, of conditions that violated every sacred principle of free government which men had shed blood to obtain." Out of loyalty to his father, Austen refuses to let his name go before the convention, but he says that it does not matter, for railroad power is doomed. The book closes with a purple passage in which Austen and Victoria tell their love to each other and watch the sunset over the river.

Harvey Sayler relates his rise to boss of the Republican Party in David Graham Phillips' *The Plum Tree* (1905). His springboard is a combine, financed by a dozen companies forming the Power Trust in his own midwestern state, which will establish its own control over the state legislature rather than dealing through middlemen such as Bill Dominick, brutal saloonkeeper and politician. By placing his own men in key positions and corporation-control statutes on the state books, Sayler makes the combine completely his own. After using this combination to ruin a rebellious "robber baron," Sayler's rule is unquestioned. He becomes a presidentmaker, later allowing his creature to return to political obscurity as the price for revolt against his authority. A penitent widower at the book's end, he is accepted by his scrupulous childhood sweetheart.

Jack London: Marxism v. Fascism, Early Phase

Jack London's *The Iron Heel* (1908) is unique for three reasons. It is one of the first relatively modern American novels which preaches Marxism, warns against Fascism, and is set in the future. Set in the twenty-seventh century, four hundred years after the Brotherhood of Man had overthrown the three-century-old Oligarchy, the novel is the annotated manuscript of Avis Everhard. The wife of Socialist leader Ernest Everhard, she is executed with him after the failure of the Second Revolt, which appears to have occurred sometime after 1918. A revolutionary Socialist, London attacked the capitalistic system, making its corporations the founders of the ruthless and repressive Oligarchy. London produces quotations from Calhoun, Lincoln, and Theodore Roosevelt warning against the domination of corporations. He describes the police and strike-breaking functions of the Pinkertons in their service, specifically names eleven industrial groups said to dominate the United States in 1907, and chronicles the efforts of the labor movements for better working conditions. Sometimes maudlin and at other times vituperative, London nevertheless gives a frightening vision of a totalitarian state such as that which later became the actuality described in Silone's novels of Italy under Mussolini. London anticipates other novels of this type even in particulars, as in the case of his "people of the abyss," who are purposely degraded and brutalized quite as much as Orwell's Proles.

James L. Ford, Samuel H. Adams, and Upton Sinclair: Oil Men and Anarchists

James L. Ford's *Hot Corn Ike* (1923) deals with political corruption in New York City, at the same time harking back through one of its characters to the Know-Nothing Party and the assassination of Bill Poole. In 1926 Samuel Hopkins Adams' *Revelry* moved on to corruption on the national scene. The novel is a *roman à clef* whose characters have a one-for-one correspondence to the real ones in Sinclair's *Oil!* Willis Markham is Warren Harding; Dan Lurcock is Barney Brockway; Anderson Gandy is Senator Crisby. If the reader likes, he can read the latter as a key to the former. Sinclair inundates the reader with a detailed account of the corruption of the Harding era and highlights of the labor movement. He treats the impact of the Russian Revolution upon America and the political implications of American troops fighting the Bolsheviks in Siberia. Following the activities of the I.W.W., he describes the resistance to them which included such measures as California's Criminal Syndicalism Act. This big book also treats, with the solidity Masters probably meant to achieve, an equally turbulent era in American national development. In *Boston* Sinclair used even more documentation to relate what he saw as the struggle between capital and labor. Through Bartolomeo Vanzetti's active career and subsequent struggle for life, the reader meets many of the militant groups in the labor movement in America during the second and third decades of this century. The I.W.W. appears again with anarcho-syndicalists, and *anarchistas*. Sinclair even distinguishes the *communisti anarchici* from the *anarchico individualista*. Although the book's literary merits are submerged by the pamphleteering and passion, it is worth reading for the slice of faintly fictionalized American political history which it presents.

John Dos Passos and James T. Farrell: Communist Infiltration

Like Steinbeck's *In Dubious Battle*, Dos Passos' *Adventures of a Young Man* deals with Communist infiltration of the American labor movement in the thirties. Giving the reader background material on the militant role of the I.W.W., both novels follow Communist labor organizers into the field among migrant agricultural workers, miners, and industrial workers. Through their characters the novelists reveal not only the immediate goals of the organizers in terms of wages and working conditions, but also the place of these struggles in the plan for a socialistic society. Dos Passos goes even farther in showing the international aspect of these efforts—the sensitivity to the Moscow-formed party line, the submergence of local issues in terms of the overall revolutionary policy.

In 1952 James T. Farrell published a novel which also dealt with Communism in the mid-thirties. It was *Yet Other Waters*, the story of Bernard Carr's attraction to Marxism and his subsequent break with it. This sometimes turgid book centers around the relation of the writer to the Communist movement. Many of the phenomena of the period are there: the magazines purveying a Marxist interpretation of literature, the writers' councils and congresses, the attempts to generate a party literature. Never a member of the Party, Carr is torn between an attraction to its stated aims and repulsion at its rigid control of thought and art. He joins picket lines, reads a paper at a Congress, and then sees the Communists turn a Socialist meeting into a riot. When he breaks with his party friends, he is given "the treatment." He is vilified in the left wing papers and reviews as party hacks make a concerted attempt to destroy his literary reputation. (And, of course, this attempted destruction of his means of livelihood is the same method used by the extreme Right to punish political divergency in *The Troubled Air* and *Stranger Come Home*.) Unfortunately, the charge that Farrell has a tin ear in writing dialogue is true. This long book has a considerable cumulative effect, but one pays for it by wading through many slow-moving passages. On the whole, though, it is a convincing portrait in depth, valuable also for its retroactive anticipation of the so-called "Literature of Disillusionment" which was to come from such writers as Silone and Koestler.

Like Hemingway's *For Whom the Bell Tolls*, Dos Passos' *Adventures of a Young Man* had in its later sections described the fight against Fascism in the Spanish Civil War. Both novels recorded the infiltration of the Loyalist forces by the Communists and the supremacy which they achieved in many sectors. In his next book, *Number One*, Dos Passos turned his attention to a source of growing concern to many Americans: dictatorship on the state level as exemplified by the Long machine in Louisiana. Two other novels, Adria Locke Langley's *A Lion Is in the Streets* (1945) and Robert Penn Warren's *All the King's Men* (1946), are similar to it, although the quality of the writing varies greatly. Dos Passos's style is characteristically dispassionate and panoramic. Warren's book, despite devices smacking of melodrama, has sweep and a highly evocative poetic prose. Langley's novel is full of worn devices: the faithful mammy with the corn-pone accent, the deathbed message, hidden documents, and a shadowy avenger. But all three books have their primary historical source in the career of Huey Long or the forces in American political life which he typified.

Upton Sinclair and John Dos Passos: Global War and Politics

In *Presidential Agent* (1945), as in the rest of the voluminous Lanny Budd series, Upton Sinclair mixed imaginary characters with real ones, and fictitious events with those from last year's newspapers. In this novel (for which any other of the series might be substituted for the present purpose), Lanny moves among the great ones of the world as their intimate and confidant. As Presidential Agent 103 with the code name Zaharoff, he sends his reports directly to President Roosevelt. Using his entree as an art expert, he further ingratiates himself into the confidence of the leading Nazis by becoming Hitler's *Kunstsachverständiger*. In this role he goes to Austria ostensibly to purchase paintings for Hitler but actually to gauge Austria's mood and its ripeness for *anschluss* with Germany. The incredible Lanny breaks into an SS dungeon, Indian-wrestles with Rudolph Hess, and briefs everyone about everyone else, from Lord Runciman to Kurt Schuschnigg. He also finds time to outline Roosevelt's Chicago "quarantine" speech. All is revealed to him, from the Cagoulard conspiracy in France to the temper of the Cliveden set in England. The pages of this long novel are jammed with events and people who made news on three continents immediately before and after Munich. A journalistic, omniscient book, *Presidential Agent* is loaded with slang, clichés, and gauche conversation and narration. But it is an outstanding example of the novel which records current political history.

Dos Passos's *Grand Design* pulls together the threads of several current themes. In this one book, the reader finds a continuation of earlier material about Communism in America, the rising labor movement, and new liberalism in government. The transition is then made to World War II, America's world responsibilities, growing recognition of the Communist threat, and American obligations in the post-war world. The novel's characters work out their individual destinies against a background of New Deal reforms and international events leading to war. But there is no arbitrary interlarding of the two. Dos Passos ably manipulates these two types of material. He weaves them together into one fabric so that they combine into a meaningful pattern which sets off individual action against group action. The NRA, the WPB, the fall of the Low Countries, the agitation for a second front—all of them are there. But in this artistic fusion the lives of Millard Carroll, Paul Graves, and Georgia Washburn remain individual, retaining their identity and meaning.

Post-War Directions

In the post-war years, the American political novel seems to have gone not in one direction but in three. The first is toward concern for America's world role as seen in *Grand Design*. The second returns to the theme of corruption. The third leads to an exploration of domestic dangers to traditional American freedoms. Weller's *The Crack in the Column* pursues the international theme, indirectly indicating, upon the basis of lessons learned in Greece, the program which has resulted in the building of American air bases from Spain to Yugoslavia. Weller's book is also valuable as a political history of wartime and postwar Greece. Besides the working of the wartime EAM front, the novel describes the pattern of planned Communist expansion and Western moves made to counteract it. Gallico's *Trial by Terror*, besides being an instrument for criticism of the foreign policy which gave no protection to American citizens jailed and tortured behind the Iron Curtain, also records one tactic of the cold war deliberately intended to ruin American prestige in Europe.

Three recent novels treat corruption on the local level. They are Charles Francis Coe's *Ashes* (1952), Mary Anne Amsbarry's *Caesar's Angel* (1952), and William Manchester's *The City of Anger* (1953). Although the theme is old, some of the actors are new. The lobbies and trusts have been replaced by a more sinister operative—the gangster. And the power behind the city government is not a single gang led by a "Little Caesar." In *Ashes* it is the Mafia, a transplanted Sicilian terrorist society. In *Caesar's Angel* the ruler is a national syndicate. The hero of *Ashes* is given a short lecture on the economics of the ring:

It is no longer possible for our interests to keep all their money profitably occupied. It piles up too fast. It threatens to become visible to the Federal taxing authorities. We are constantly seeking, and finding, new areas in which to invest. So-called legitimate areas. It is foolhardy, perhaps, to pay such taxes as legitimate commerce requires, but our sums are so vast that our interests feel that they should be converted into capital assets.

The scale of corruption in Manchester's book is more modest, for there the rotten façade has been undermined by a local numbers racket rather than a national group. The bought politicians are clearly drawn, as are the agents who subvert them. Once again we are dealing with fiction, but we need only turn to the findings of state and federal commissions of inquiry to see the bases in fact. The best of these rather ordinary novels is *The City of Anger*. The Freudian critic will be interested in Manchester's recurrent images of decay, corruption, and physical filth which may, however, represent an attempt to buttress stylistically his basic theme of political and moral corruption. In *Caesar's Angel* Mrs. Amsbarry's criminals and police are terribly hard-boiled but not completely convincing. Although her gangsters are much better done than Mrs. Langley's in *A Lion Is in the Streets*, she still sounds somehow like a very nice lady trying to be very tough. With his clipped, repetitive sentences and grim-jawed men, Coe seems to be suffering from an overdose of Hemingway. Yet at times he manages to go one hundred and eighty degrees in the opposite direction with dialogue like this from "Young Tim": "You alone, Mums, combine such true goodness of soul with such great understanding of things!"

Concern over threats to personal freedom forms the basis for Shaw's *The Troubled Air* and Shirer's *Stranger Come Home*. The events and characters in these novels make it clear that they too have as their starting points the contemporary history which they cloak in fiction. The blacklists of Shaw's book are as real as Shirer's Senator O'Brien and his Senate Committee on Security and Americanism. Shirer's people are taken from contemporary American life. Across his stage parade General Cyrus Field Clark, a newspaper chain owner of medieval prejudices and keeper of faded ex-movie star Madeleine Marlowe; Bert Woodruff, a demented columnist; William McKinley Forbes, dictatorial tobacco tycoon; and Senator Reynolds, the committee's representative from the Old South. The supporting roles are filled with the same accuracy. They include the professional ex-Communists and the sharp little committee counsel who puts loaded questions with ominous mentions of perjury. The commentator's radio career is destroyed like that of his Foreign Service friend, although both are innocent men. Shirer ranges far afield, from comments upon similar periods of "hysteria" in American history to Hollywood's refusal to film *Hiawatha* because his "peace efforts might be regarded as Red propaganda." The plight of Whitehead is well imagined, but the book's diary form is not a particularly happy choice and much of its prose is awkward. As a record of the source of some of the most spectacular domestic news of recent years, however, the novel is worth reading.

Mailer's *Barbary Shore*, which is not a part of any of the three post-war trends, displays the novelist's function as a historian in its retelling of the story of the Russian Revolution. A twenty-page account and eulogy are followed by a description of the revolution's failure to spread and its consequent nationalization. Lovett also recounts his discipleship under Trotsky before he goes on to list the forces which created a police state instead of a promised land.

THE CONTINENT AND ELSEWHERE

Joseph Conrad: Colonial Politics and Revolution

Joseph Conrad's *Nostromo* (1904) may be read as a history if one interprets it as a typical case of government-making by foreign industrial interests in late-nineteenth-century South America. With the American Holroyd as his silent partner and financial backer, British-educated Charles Gould uses the wealth of his San Tomas silver mine to finance the successful revolt of Occidental Province from the Republic of Costaguana, which is in the grip of the tyrannical Montero brothers. A good deal of actual history is injected through the reminiscences of old Giorgio Viola, who had fought under Garibaldi across South America to Italy. But it was in *The Secret Agent* and *Under Western Eyes* that Conrad recorded more memorable history. Both books give extensive accounts of revolutionary and counter-revolutionary activities. A superb artist, Conrad did not need to go to a series of actual events and people. His imaginative synthesis of the factors which produce them created, however, a true pattern of this whole complex of revolutionary activity. Besides the sensitive exploration of the characters of Razumov, Nathalia, and Victorovitch, one finds actions which characterized the movement in which they were swept up. Conrad presents the espionage and counterespionage, the bomb plots, and the abortive revolts. Though he wrote out of revulsion at revolutionary activity, his point of view did not blind him to the miseries of Czarist Russia. With artistic integrity, he described the repressive commissions, their imprisonments, exiles, and executions. His account of the fate of Mikulin, chief of Czarist counterespionage, makes extremely interesting reading in 1954. For Mikulin one could almost substitute Koestler's Rubashov:

Later on, the larger world first heard of him in the very hour of his downfall, during one of those State trials which astonish and puzzle the average man who reads the newspapers by a glimpse of unsuspected intrigues. And in the stir of vaguely seen monstrosities, in that momentary, mysterious disturbance of muddy waters, Councilor Mikulin went under, dignified, with only a calm, emphatic protest of his innocence—nothing more. No disclosures damaging to a harassed autocracy, complete fidelity to the secret of the miserable *arcana imperii*, deposited in his patriotic breast a display of bureaucratic stoicism in a Russian official's ineradicable, almost sublime contempt for truth; stoicism of silence understood only by very few of the initiated, and not without a certain cynical grandeur of self-sacrifice on the part of a Sybarite. For the terribly heavy sentence turned Councilor Mikulin civilly into a corpse, and actually into something very much like a common convict.

It seems that the savage autocracy, any more than the divine democracy, does not limit its diet exclusively to the bodies of its enemies. It devours its friends and servants as well.

The Soviet State: Its Roots and Growth

It was this same Czarist Russia of which Turgenev wrote in *Fathers and Sons*. Examining Nihilism, he also looked at contemporary events such as the emancipation of serfs and the attempts of some landowners to improve the lot of their workers despite agrarian disturbances. Violently anti-revolutionary, Dostoyevsky replied in *The Possessed* to what appeared to him to be Turgenev's advocacy of revolution. In his massive and powerful novel he showed the agitation produced by groups such as the "quintets" organized by Pytor Verhovensky, themselves the forerunners of the Communist cells.

In Koestler's *Darkness at Noon* Dostoyevsky's nightmare becomes an even more terrible actuality. In his introductory note Koestler writes:

The characters in this book are fictitious. The historical circumstances which determined their actions are real. The life of the man N. S. Rubashov is a synthesis of the lives of a number of men who were victims of the so-called Moscow Trials. Several of them were personally known to the author. This book is dedicated to their memory.

Through flashbacks the reader sees Stalin, Lenin, and the members of the First International Congress. Not only does he witness the breaking of Rubashov for his trial, but also the series of cold and merciless acts of expediency which have eroded the soul of the old Bolshevik and left him ready for his final service to the Party. Koestler describes the agonizing process by which the confession is extracted. Gletkin, his interrogator, supplies the rationale for the whole performance and for most of the repressive acts of the state as well. In some ways, Rubashov is reminiscent of Trotsky, with his pince-nez, his record as a commander in the Revolution, his extensive service outside Russia, and his onetime rank as a top Communist. (A closer resemblance to Trotsky is that of the Party's fictitious scapegoat in 1984. Emmanuel Goldstein, with his fuzzy hair and small goatee, is the arch-counterrevolutionary, the author of *The Theory and Practice of Oligarchical Collectivism*.) *Darkness at Noon* is a stark and brilliant book. Artistically satisfying, it also presents a record of a characteristic phenomenon of Russian Communism.

Marie-Henri Beyle [Stendhal]: Napoleonic Panorama

Thirty-nine years after he followed Napoleon's armies into Italy, Stendhal published a sweeping novel of that era. *The Charterhouse of Parma* follows the career of Fabrizio Valserra, Marchesino del Dongo, from birth to death. It shows the influence upon his life of his beautiful, devoted, and scheming aunt, the Contessa Gina Pietranera. We meet her lover, Conte Mosca della Rovere Sorezana, Minister to Prince Ernesto IV of Parma and politician extraordinary, and become privy to the intrigues of the court. This large novel is crammed with incident—duels, assignations, affairs, prison-breaks, and even the assassination of a monarch. Besides all this, Stendhal relates some of the major events in French and Italian history during nearly thirty years. In particular, we see Napoleon's triumphal entries into Italy in 1796, 1801, and 1815. Fabrizio even participates on the fringes of the battle of Waterloo. With each arrival and departure, Napoleon's adherents and those of the Austrian Emperor play musical chairs for the positions of power. Even after Napoleon has been banished to Elba a struggle goes on between Liberals (or Jacobins) and the proponents of absolute monarchy. The Liberal cause is perverted in Parma by the rascally General Fabio Conti, who ironically serves as Ernesto's political jailer, but the temper of this movement in Europe is reflected in the thoughts and actions of many of the characters. Describing authoritarian government and the struggles against it, as well as the interrelation of a corrupt church and a corrupt state, Stendhal's classic successfully fuses the lives of his people with the times in which they lived.

André Malraux: Comintern v. Kuomintang

Nearly a hundred years later André Malraux wrote of a time of political chaos in *Man's Fate*. But the span of his novel was four months rather than thirty years. Malraux gives a detailed account of Chiang Kai-shek's military victory of 1927 in Shanghai and his subsequent crushing of the Chinese Communist forces which fought him. Not only does he examine the roles of the immediate participants—the White Guards, the governmental army, the "Reds" and "Blues" of the Kuomintang—but also the intervention of outside forces as well—the Russian Communists, the Shanghai bankers, the French Chamber of Commerce, and the Franco-Asiatic Consortium. Malraux explores both the military and economic aspects of the struggle. Kyo Gisors feels that triumph here will mean "the U.S.S.R. increased to six hundred million men." Ferral, head of the Chamber and the Consortium, realizes that it will also mean the end of his group's commercial penetration of the Yangtze basin. *Man's Fate* may be read for these insights into the uprising of 1927 and also for background on the formulation of the Communist decision which kept the armies of Mao Tse-tung, Chu Teh, and others within the Kuomintang until they gained enough strength to defeat it.

Jean-Paul Sartre: The Shadow of Munich

Jean-Paul Sartre's technique in *The Reprieve* (1947) may remind one of a photographer whose camera mechanism has gone awry. What he is trying to do is clear, but it does not quite come off. Covering the week of September 23–30, 1938, the novel is kaleidoscopic. Using more than nine distinct couples or groups, Sartre jumps from the activities of one to another with no transition. The scene may change from sentence to sentence or even within a sentence. He obviously does this to portray events which are happening simultaneously. He also uses this technique, apparently, to give some sense of the chaos that reigned during the week when Europe was on the verge of war. To show the impact of these events upon France, he has selected his people from many strata of French society. Interspersed between all these semi-fragmented stories and incidents are dialogues between the politicians: Hitler and his aides, Daladier and Bonnet, Chamberlain and Halifax, Sir Nevile Henderson and Sir Horace Wilson. Through its characters the novel ranges over Europe from England to the Sudetenland, finally arriving at Munich. The book's last two paragraphs serve as an example of this technique which has a cumulative effect but which can be extremely troublesome to a reader accustomed to conventional narration. Daladier's plane lands at Le Bourget as Milan Hlinka, a loyal Sudeten Czech, hears of his country's dismemberment:

A vast clamor greeted [Daladier], the crowd surged through the cordon of police and swept the barriers away; Milan drank and said with a laugh: "To France! To England! To our glorious allies!" Then he flung the glass against the wall; they shouted: "Hurrah for France! Hurrah for England! Hurrah for peace!" They were carrying flags and flowers. Daladier stood on the top step and looked at them dumbfounded. Then he turned to Leger and said between his teeth: "The God-damned fools!"

Fascism through Italian Eyes

Collectively, the novels of Ezio Taddei, Alberto Moravia, and Ignazio Silone present a history of Italy during the years that saw Mussolini's rise, reign, and ruin. Taddei's *The Pine Tree and the Mole* (1945) is set in

Livorno in 1919. On one social level the novel follows the career of Michele Pellizari, whose political odyssey leads him from the Italian Socialist Party to the Fascist Party, and eventually to a return to the land of his peasant people. On another level the novel relates the rise of Rubachiuchi from jail-bird to Fascist *agent provocateur* and party official. There are many long passages throughout the book in which Taddei drops his characters to go directly to a recital of the events which led to the triumph of the Fascists. He describes the return of war veterans filled with unrest and plagued with unemployment. He records the failure of the Socialists as the Fascists deliberately fill their Black Shirt squads with convicted criminals. He sets down the workers' capture of the factories and finally the Fascist march on Rome.

In *The Conformist* (1951) Alberto Moravia is more concerned with a psychological portrait of Marcello Clerici than he is with the description of the period. But in analyzing the trauma-inspired desire for conformity which led to his job in Mussolini's secret police, Moravia tells a good deal about the political climate of Italy of yesterday—from the palmy days of the Ethiopian campaign to the time of the retribution which leaves Marcello and his family dead by the roadside from the bullets of a strafing Allied plane.

Three of Ignazio Silone's powerful novels, *Fontamara*, *Bread and Wine*, and *A Handful of Blackberries*, deal with Italian political history from the middle thirties to the years immediately following World War II. Writing from exile when the Fascists were in power, Silone consistently dealt with the repression of the Italian peasant. Although he always focuses on small places such as Fontamara, Pietrasecca, and San Luca, his characters are in a sense generic, representing the non-Fascists who want only enough bread and wine to live life decently with a little comfort and security. Silone describes the regimentation of Italian life in the city as well as the village. He also shows, as does Koestler in *Darkness at Noon*, the destruction of the Communist Party after the rise to power of a dictatorship of the Right. *A Handful of Blackberries* has as its background the resurgence of the Italian Communist Party after the fall of Mussolini. But Silone preserves a continuity with his earlier books by a continuing account of the struggle of the peasants against the landed families. In this book the Tarocchi family is the equivalent of Prince Torlonia in *Fontamara*. Fascism has been crushed, but the great landowner is still the force which the peasant must fight to keep his small plot.

Alan Paton: The Trek of the Boers

Alan Paton's *Cry, the Beloved Country* and *Too Late the Phalarope* detail the bases of South Africa's explosive contemporary political life. The anti-Negro legislation, the segregation, the police control of the native peoples are all set forth. Paton's moving novels record the individual tragedies which transpire in this climate of tears and violence. They also show their historical antecedents. The red flashes which Peter Van

Vlaanderen wore on his shoulders during the war meant that he would fight anywhere in Africa. To some this made him

a Smuts man, a traitor to the language and struggle of the Afrikaner people, and a lickspittle of the British Empire and the English King, fighting in an English war that no true Afrikaner would take part in.

Here is a historical fact that illustrates the division between the peoples of South Africa. Another is the Immorality Act of 1927, which typifies another great source of conflict and causes Pieter's ruin.

Richard Kaufmann: The Third Reich

Richard Kaufmann's *Heaven Pays No Dividends* (1951) is one of the better books to come out of post-war Germany although it is not, as its cover enthusiastically declares, the "modern *All Quiet on the Western Front*." Roderich Stamm is a completely non-political young art historian who drifts into Nazi organizations because life is made rather unpleasant for one outside them. His father, however, is an economist who becomes attracted to the Nazi movement, lectures at meetings, and eventually rises to an important post in Hitler's Foreign Ministry. As a gunner in a flak battery, Stamm fights in France, Russia, and Germany. He emerges from the war minus several teeth, an arm, and all his illusions. Each of the girls he has loved has married or died. Through his eyes the reader sees the events leading to victory in Paris and defeat on the road from Stalingrad. But one also meets Gestapo men like Alfred Karawan and officials like Heinrich Himmler. This novel chronicles the sound and fury of politics and war as it explores the effects on the German people of the rise and fall of the Third Reich. Less political than most novels in this study, Kaufmann's book has a good deal in common with many of them. The lives of its people are played out against a backdrop of local, national, and international affairs. And the novelist records not only the comings and goings of the individuals he creates, but also the events of the world in which they live.

chapter four

The Novel as Mirror of National Character

A political novel invariably reveals the attitude of its author toward the national groups from which its characters come. Often the author may seek to draw a national portrait by describing political behavior which he believes is peculiarly characteristic of Spaniards or Greeks or Englishmen. Two novels which thus portray the Russians are *Under Western Eyes* and *The Possessed*. The reader may work with a body of novels which do not deliberately attempt to delineate national character, and yet he will still arrive at some conception of national behavior patterns. He can do this by assessing the subjects treated. If most of the novels deal with underground activities, *coups d'état*, or revolutions, he is justified in assuming that this is a people which takes its politics seriously, and emotionally. If most of the novels concern parliamentary give and take, clever use of rules, strategic marches and countermarches, he has a right to conclude that this national group has achieved some degree of political sophistication. In dealing with the American novel one has to draw conclusions in this way. There is a great deal of close attention to tactical and strategic moves, but there is not too much scrutiny of larger behavior patterns. The appraiser must use whatever materials seem capable of giving insight: detailed discussion which is precisely in point, a recurrent basic situation, or a group of themes whose frequency of appearance is a good indication of their importance and relevance.

Enough American and English novels are included here to justify drawing some conclusions. Some of the other national literatures discussed, however, are represented by relatively few books. Since they constitute a small sample, one can draw only tentative conclusions. But almost all these novels are by very talented writers whose work is considered representative of the best in this genre within their national literatures. They are novels which offer skilled portrayals of life by artists entitled to a hearing on their own merits. In order to extract as much from the novel as possible in this area, comments on nations have been accepted from foreigners where they seem valid.

GREAT BRITAIN: A SELF-PORTRAIT

Peaceful Change in the Political Realm

The English political novel presents a people whose political processes have operated in a well-defined manner with progressively decreasing

violence. England had its Wars of the Roses and its Cavaliers and Round-
heads, but with the exception of the Jacobite Rebellion of 1746, resort
to arms as a means of domestic change has been in the discard for the
past two hundred years of English history. The Peterloo Massacre, the
Chartist Riots, and the struggle against the Lords all involved bloodshed,
but this form of conflict has largely subsided. The novel reflects this pattern. It is one of change within a framework of relative stability. The Right
wing and the Left are the two poles between which the political ions flow.
The names of the poles may vary, as may some of the elements in their
chemical composition, but their function remains the same. The Tory is
always the opponent of change or the advocate of slow and minimal change;
the Whig, Liberal, Fabian, or Labourite is the champion of more rapid
and extensive change. The extreme radical appears occasionally, the revolutionary infrequently. Almost all the English novels in this study show this
basic alignment. Even when the liberals are represented by Mrs. Ward's
Venturists and the conservatives by Disraeli's Young Englanders or Wells's
New Tories, this is the essential political structure. George Eliot's Felix
Holt and Harold Transome, both Radicals, are set off against the Debarry
family headed by Parson Jack and Sir Maximus Debarry. Meredith's Nevil
Beauchamp is another young Radical in conflict with his uncle Everard
Romfrey, who calls himself a Whig but is an aristocratic reactionary. Except for Disraeli, James, and Conrad, the authors of these novels tend to
present the case of the liberal or progressive. But no matter what the point
of view or time, the main characters tend to range themselves on one of
these two sides.

Conrad's *The Secret Agent* departs from the common liberal-conservative
alignment by dealing with the dangerous lunatic fringe of English political
life—the revolutionary terriorists. But Verloc, the novel's main character,
and Yundt, one of the most violent members of the circle, are not native
Englishmen. In using these characters, Conrad views the same political
virtues the other novelists treat by contrasting them with violence. When
the embassy secretary orders Verloc to blow up the Greenwich Observatory,
he tells him that the English must be shocked into repressive action. "This
country," he says, "is absurd with its sentimental regard for individual
liberty." The Professor, "The Perfect Anarchist," attempts to goad Police
Inspector Heat into seizing him when they meet in an alley. Heat knows
that if he does so the Professor will blow both of them up by pressing
the detonator in his pocket. Undoubtedly this fact crosses his mind, but
his answer is typical: "If I were to lay my hand on you now I would be
no better than yourself."

The Englishman's often unemotional approach to politics also appears
in the novels. In *The New Machiavelli*, Dick Remington, enthusiastic about
Socialism and "the working-man," is one of a group of students who invite
Chris Robinson, "the Ambassador of the Workers," to Cambridge to talk
to them. But when Robinson speaks, they are disappointed at the excess
of emotion and deficiency of content. When the Englishman does allow

emotion to surge into his politics, it may be mixed with religion. It was said of Hamer Shawcross, in *Fame Is the Spur*, that "his platform manner was that of a revivalist parson." Chester Nimmo has somewhat the same style in *Prisoner of Grace*. A former Wesleyan lay-preacher, he advocates pacifism at one point in his career. His wife Nina comments:

to a man like Chester, whose politics were mixed up with religion and whose religion was always getting into his politics, this was the situation which he was accustomed to handle. It did not prevent his religion from being "true" that he knew how to "use" it.

Both these politicians are liberals, and perhaps this is merely another means of separating the two great groups. The university man, who has had some advantages, may look upon emotionalism as bad form; the working man, for whom grade school and the church often constitute his only sources of formal education, is conditioned to respond to the stimuli he has known in one of these institutions: the emotional approach of the revivalist parson or the lay preacher.

Despite the reaction of the aristocrats to this lower group, some of the English novelists regard them as a great source of national strength. Disraeli may have felt that they needed guidance, not freedom and self-expression; Orwell found hope in them. Looking out the window of his and Julia's rendezvous, Winston Smith sees the figure of a woman of the Proles, a "solid, unconquerable figure, made monstrous by work and childbearing, toiling from birth to death and still singing. Out of those mighty loins a race of conscious beings must one day come."

The Fruits of Imperialism

When one thinks of the literature of imperialism he is likely to remember Kipling's *Soldiers Three*, *Mandalay*, or *Recessional*. Wells's Dick Remington remarks, "The prevailing force in my undergraduate days was not Socialism but Kiplingism." But if Kipling emphasizes the White Man's Burden, most other novelists emphasize the White Man's Guilt. In *Beauchamp's Career* Col. Halkett looks up from his newspaper to remark to Nevil, "There's an expedition against the hill-tribes in India, and we're a peaceful nation, eh? We look as if we were in for a complication with China." And Nevil replies ironically, "Well, sir, we must sell our opium." Forster's *A Passage to India* lays prime responsibility for India's tragedy at Britain's doorstep. He pictures the cruel clannishness and snobbery of the English colony of Chandrapore with its Mrs. Callendar who declares, "Why, the kindest thing one can do to a native is to let him die." India is full of red-faced Ronny Heaslops, officials who play God, a god whose thunderbolts and lightnings are infantry, cavalry, and artillery. Mrs. Moore, the single English subject in Chandrapore able to bridge the enormous gap between the two cultures, reflects about Ronny:

One touch of regret—not the canny substitute but the true regret from the heart—would have made him a different man, and the British Empire a different institution.

There is no question in this novel that Britain is the violator in this loveless union. The South African novels recall Wordsworth's line about the makers of the French Revolution "become oppressors in their turn." The Afrikaners may now be the malefactors; at one time they, like the Indians, were clearly the victims. Jakob Van Vlaanderen, the great stern patriarch of *Too Late the Phalarope*, recalls the trek into the interior to escape the repressive measures of the British. Jim Latter in *Prisoner of Grace* travels to London from Nigeria, where he has overseen the destinies of a tribe for years, because he is convinced that the people in the Colonial Office "want to kill off the Lugas."

As Britain began to exchange the imperialist role for that of co-defender of the West, this deftness and high-handedness in international affairs was sometimes regarded as an asset. Major Walker assesses it for Tommy Mc-Phail in *The Crack in the Column* when he says, "You're no match for us in arranging a chain of political events, in planning several moves ahead, in making the baby be born exactly when the horoscope says, sex, weight, and appearance of innocence guaranteed."

Like any good national literature, the English turns inward the searching light of criticism. The reader sees hypocrites, time-servers, and turncoats. Spread before him are domestic abuses and cold imperialism. But he is also given a glimpse of a people who retain a regard for the rights and dignity of the individual, a people who have turned away from violence and shown a remarkable capacity for achieving change without sacrificing stability, for combining growth with order.

THE UNITED STATES: A SELF-PORTRAIT

De Forest, in *Playing the Mischief*, describes Congressman Sykes Drummond as a "Robert-the-Devil" type. This complete cynic makes an interesting comment on the conditions around him: "A John Bull told me yesterday that there is no such thing known in England as a municipal ring or a thieving mayor. That is what any American of the present day would set down as a fairy story." If the political novel has any validity as a commentary on national characteristics, one conclusion is inescapable: many Americans become criminals when they accept public office. Drummond's comment is borne out by the two groups of novels. In the English novel individuals such as Hamer Shawcross and Chester Nimmo sell out to the opposition. Nimmo even engages in commercial activities too closely related to his official duties to be quite proper. But there is a complete absence of the corruption portrayed at all levels of government in the American political novel.

Crawford attempted to differentiate the English from the American early in *An American Politician*. The novel's political naïveté renders any of its judgments suspect, but in this Crawford appears to come close to the truth. His opinion is that

English people . . . love to associate with persons of rank and power from a disinterested love of these things themselves, whereas in most other countries the society of notable and influential persons is chiefly sought from the most cynical motives of personal advantage. . . . But politics in England and politics in America, so far as the main points are concerned, are as different as it is possible for any two social functions to be. Roughly, Government and the doings of Government are centripetal in England, and centrifugal in America. In England the will of the people assists the working of Providence, whereas in America, devout persons pray that Providence may on occasion modify the will of the people. In England men believe in the Queen, the Royal Family, the Established Church, and Belgravia first, and in themselves afterwards. Americans believe in themselves devoutly, and a man who could "establish" upon them a church, a royalty, or a peerage, would be a very clever fellow.

His diagnosis of cynicism and self-interest as leading American characteristics is echoed in the other novels. Good politicians do appear, but for every Lincoln there are ten Boss Tweeds. Henry Adams' *Democracy* also contains passages in which American political life is compared unfavorably with that of England. Madeleine Lee attends an immensely boring White House reception. Not only are the guests dull, but to her the President and his wife appear as automatons aping royalty.

Forces of Corruption

Complete responsibility for corruption does not always rest with the politician. Some office holders, like Honest John Vane, sincerely try to stay clean. The corrupt politician usually has a collaborator in the person of the man who buys him. In Garland's *A Spoil of Office* Bradley Talcott's illusions are shattered in the legislature and in Congress. Looking around him he finds that "to rob the commonwealth was a joke." State legislatures are often described as assemblages of brigands. The "Woodchuck Session" of the legislature in *Coniston* is arrant banditry, and the ones in *The Plum Tree* and *Mr. Crewe's Career* are only a little less obvious. The industrialist is usually co-villain with his politician hireling. When he does not appear in person, he is represented by his middleman, the professional lobbyist. The lobbyist's unscrupulous use of his trusting wife is the subject of Frances Hodgson Burnett's *Through One Administration* (1914). Jacob Pike, in *Playing the Mischief*, regards the institution with pride:

From his point of view, it was a kind of public life; it was more completely "inside politics" than even electioneering or legislation; it was, as he believed, the very germ and main-spring of statesmanship. A leading lobbyist knew exactly how the world is governed, and for what purpose . . .

This whole aspect of the American governmental process in the novel is a very unsavory one. The industrialists are predatory robber barons who purchase dishonest politicians in order to obtain special privilege. In *The Charterhouse of Parma* the Contessa dissuades Fabrizio from going to America by explaining to him "the cult of the god *Dollar*." In several of his novels Sinclair declares that American foreign policy has been determined by the industrial interests. He portrays Dollar Diplomacy with a vengeance. In *Oil!* he contends that the United States joined with Britain and France to fight the Bolsheviks not because of political ideology, but because "the creditor nations meant to make an example of Soviet Russia, and establish the rule that a government which repudiated its debts would be put out of business." He also tells the reader that the same oil interests which backed Harding had turned in and out of office a succession of Mexican governments to suit their own commercial purposes. And it is not hard to see in *Nostromo* the influence of the American tycoon Holroyd at work when the American cruiser *Powhatan* appears to salute the Occidental flag and "put an end to the Costaguana-Sulaco War."

If the perverters of power are not demagogues with messianic complexes, they may be gangsters who rule by ballots when bribery fails. These subjects in the novel did not go out of vogue with the Muckraking Era or with Prohibition. A new rash of novels about gangsters in politics has appeared in recent years. The gunman who is concerned about investing his money may be replacing the one who writes his name with machine gun bullets, but his influence in politics is the same.

The American Idealist

The reverse side of this particular coin shows the idealist at work. He may come out of the political wringer with his ideals mangled and his illusions full of holes, but still he retains something of the impulse which created the Declaration of Independence and the Constitution. Millard Carroll in *The Grand Design* is such a one, but he emerges as an old man at the end of his ordeal. Nick Burr in Ellen Glasgow's *The Voice of the People* (1900) is another, but his end is violent death. In recent years this idealistic aspect of the American political character has often found expression in heroes who engage in the direct struggle for liberty. Both Robert Jordan and Glenn Spotswood spill their blood on Spanish earth fighting against Franco. Were it not for the crusading district attorneys of books such as *Ashes* and *Caesar's Angel*, the implication would be that the American girds on his armor abroad but avoids conflict in his own back yard. Even so, something of this impression may remain with the reader.

Responsibility at Home and Abroad

The pattern in which a nation allows its liberties to be subverted and destroyed is a familiar one. It is often thought that certain peoples, like the Germans and Russians, are more susceptible to authoritarianism than others. One stereotype of the American—descendant of Minute Men, the man who hates cops, the fan who cherishes his right to boo the umpire—has contributed to the impression that this submissiveness to authority has never been a part of the American character. Lewis's *It Can't Happen Here*, Dos Passos's *District of Columbia*, and the novels about dictators in southern states raise some doubts about the validity of this fundamental assumption. Each of these novelists seems to feel that the American citizen could well wake up one morning to find his rights gone as did the German citizen of the early thirties. Lewis dramatizes this catastrophe on a national scale, while Dos Passos, Warren, and Langley present it on the state level. Dos

Passos, all through his trilogy, writes such frequent exhortations to vigilance
that there is little doubt that he too has worries on this score. In *Stranger
Come Home* Shirer centers his fire on McCarthyism, but he also goes back
into history to recall the passage of the Alien and Sedition Acts and the
domestic anti-German violence of World War I. The popular press and
magazines may represent the American as one who hearkens to the great
voices on each Fourth of July and understands what he is doing when he
raises his banner on Flag Day. The novelist often has serious doubts that
he does.

Europeans have called the United States immature in world affairs. At
least one of the novels in this group examines this accusation, and two others
consider the same theme of irresponsibility on the national level. In both
A Fool's Errand and *Bricks Without Straw* Tourgée accused the federal
government of irresponsibility. There is a close parallel between this case
and the one Europeans have made. Pursuing an ideal, at least in part, the
United States musters its enormous industrial and economic potential, puts
its great strength into the field, and wins military victory. After talking a
great deal about what should be done, it sets up committees which write
many reports. Then the nation promptly forgets the problems of victory
and happily returns to consideration of the tariff question or who is going
to win the World Series. In the latter of his two books, Tourgée writes that
the Northern statesmen and political writers seemed always to assume that
the destruction of slavery would cure all the ills of the Negro. With a
typical flourish, he adds:

The Nation gave the jewel of liberty into the hands of the [Negroes], armed
them with the weapons of self-government, and said: "Ye are many; protect
what ye have received." Then it took away its hand, turned away its eyes, closed
its ears to every cry of protest or of agony, and said: "We will not aid you nor
protect you. Though you are ignorant, from you we will demand works of wisdom. Though you are weak, great things shall be required at your hands." Like
the ancient taskmaster, the Nation said: *"There shall no straw be given you,
yet shall ye deliver the tale of bricks."*

Nearly seventy years later, in *The Crack in the Column*, Weller said
virtually the same thing. But this time both the problem and the stakes
were global.

The picture of American politics which emerges from the political novel
is an unflattering one. Although the "smoke-filled room" may be a cliché
in the newspapers, it is a fact in the novel. The deck of candidates is
shuffled, cut, and dealt—often from the bottom. The national conventions
are a combination of circus spectacle and cynical chicanery. And after campaigns financed by funds from special interest groups, the people's chosen
representatives get down to the serious business of paying off their debts
while lining their pockets. The crusaders for liberty and justice who appear
can be set off against these political liabilities. But the electorate in whose
behalf they struggle often seems unaware of the importance of the fight.
Inheritors of a tradition of dissent and individual freedom, they are fair

game for demagogues. They are also easy marks for the revolutionaries who, for perverted purposes, exploit their sincere but naïve desire for social and economic reform. Although the Republic somehow seems to weather periods of internecine violence and reversion to authoritarian rule, its citizens have a bad case of myopia in the field of foreign affairs. There are indications, though, that the corrective lenses bought in two world wars are beginning to bring distant events into focus. The American novelist's view of his own political arena agrees surprisingly well with many foreign estimates of it. The American seems like an immature giant who tolerates much rough behavior but rushes into conflict when he feels that his basic security is threatened. Now the giant seems to be settling down. Still likely to make violent moves, he is acquiring some of the political sophistication that was, perhaps, too early expected of him.

ITALY: A SELF-PORTRAIT

After a quarrel with Jean Colbert, Tony Maggiore in *Caesar's Angel* berates her friend Al Piazza: "You talk so big about it making no difference between American and Italian girls. You ever hear a good Italian girl open her mouth about politics? You hear her insulting the men?" This assertion is contradicted by Stella in Silone's *A Handful of Blackberries*, but even were it completely true, it would be one of the minor differences between American and Italian political behavior patterns. Immensely different historical antecedents separate the two peoples. The Italian, with a background of autocratic rule except for comparatively short intervals, has played his political role on a far different stage from that of the American. But there is more to it than just politics. The economic bases which help to form political groups have produced in Italy a stratification in which the layers are more widely separated than any in America. The migrant fruit pickers, the dust-blown Okies, the exploited miners in America seem well off beside the systematically persecuted peasants and submerged city *lumpenproletariat* of Italy. The Italians at the other end of the scale are just as far from the norm. Gould, Fisk, and Vanderbilt may have owned railroads, but Prince Torlonia owns immense ranges of the Roman and Tuscan countryside, together with 35,000 acres of the Fucino basin worked by eleven thousand farmers. But this great gulf between classes is only one of the factors which appear responsible for Italy's political ills.

Silone concentrates mainly upon the peasantry in his novels. His heart is close to them, and his description is sympathetic. But he does more than set forth their sufferings. His books also diagnose the cause of their problems and suggest solutions. Many of his peasants appear like credulous, superstitious children. The four-day thunder and lightning storm which nearly sweeps Pietrasecca off its mountain in *Bread and Wine* is blamed upon two lovers who have gone to live in a house considered damned. Don Paolo watches the gathering of a crowd which is swept into such a hysteria by its roar of "CHAY DOO! CHAY DOO! CHAY DOO!" that it forgets to listen to the oracular radio voice it has come to hear. Silone pities them: "a people whose wisdom was summed up in a few proverbs passed down from generation to generation, had been literally submerged and overwhelmed by propaganda." Don Paolo also blames this ignorance upon the Church in Italy. Like his teacher Don Benedetto, who was said to have called the reigning pontiff "Pope Pontius XI," Don Paolo feels that Italy needs

A Christianity denuded of all mythology, of all theology, of all Church control; a Christianity that neither abdicates in the face of Mammon, nor proposes concordats with Pontius Pilate, nor offers easy careers to the ambitious, but rather leads to prison . . .

Silone's hero is equally dissatisfied with a religious vocation which withdraws from life. He talks with the beautiful and spiritual Christina, who devoutly waits to enter the convent:

Do you not think that this divorce between a spirituality which retires into contemplation and a mass of people dominated by animal instincts is the source of all our ills? Do you not think that every living creature ought to live and struggle among his fellow-creatures rather than shut himself up in an ivory tower?

Although *A Handful of Blackberries* contains more scenes set in Rome than the other two Silone novels discussed here, a better view of the Italian city dweller is given by Taddei and Moravia. Taddei's *The Pine Tree and the Mole* is built about citizens of Livorno who are as widely separated by wealth and position as are Silone's Old Zaccaria and the Tarocchi family. The circle of lawyers and politicians who exchange wives and party labels are a different breed of men from the jailbirds, pimps, and informers at the opposite extreme of Livorno's social structure. But both groups are equally adrift, both caught in the same wave of post-World War I exhaustion and economic derangement which sent so many Italians in search of the answer that Mussolini seemed to provide. Taddei emphasizes poverty and depression as the main factors which prepared the way for the Fascist regime, but one senses something else, particularly among his representatives of the educated class. They seem to be seeking some sort of order, a stabilizing force in their political life. Taddei says that the Italian Socialist Party seemed to offer the solution. But the Socialists failed because

overwhelmed by the favorable-seeming course of events and overlooking the most important phase of the matter, they lacked the time to think of many things and, instead, viewed the period with optimistic eyes; everything appeared to them to depend upon the number of adherents that any particular event brought into their ranks. Political expediency thus became, in a manner of speaking, epidemic, and the deepening crisis in all its amplitude became apparent in the form of a spiritual crisis that was its reflection.

Marcello Clerici in *The Conformist* finds his solution in Fascism. Taddei's hero turns at last to the same source of strength which Silone singles out—the land and its people. They both feel, rather like Orwell, that the masses are the ultimate source of their country's salvation. Old

Lazzaro, shouting defiance at the Communists, epitomizes these people: "There'll always be someone that refuses to sell his soul for a handful of beans and a piece of cheese." In this he is like Conrad's Giorgio Viola, "the Garibaldino," an old expatriate whose divinities are Garibaldi and Liberty.

This small group of Italian novelists portray their countrymen as members of widely separated economic and social classes. There are the well-to-do who seem to seek order and get it with a vengeance. And there are the poor of the cities and villages who are the victims of this order, squeezed by poverty, by powerful landowners, and harnessed by a church which renders more than is his to Caesar, a church which brings politics into the confessional and divorces religion from everyday life. Something of the spirit of Garibaldi still lives, however, nourished by the deprived ones who are close to the soil. Perhaps this is a modern political parable in which the last shall be first.

SPAIN: AN AMERICAN PORTRAIT

Robert Jordan's love of Spain is not an abstract emotion. He has a deep feeling for its people, but he is still able to see their faults. Throughout *For Whom the Bell Tolls* he makes conscious estimates of their national character. He says they are a truly thoughtful and considerate people who are not merely formally polite as are the French. But they are also treacherous:

Of course they turned on you. They turned on you often but they always turned on everyone. They turned on themselves, too. If you had three together, two would unite against one, and then the two would start to betray each other. Not always, but often enough for you to take enough cases and start to draw it as a conclusion.

These characteristics cut across party lines. The Rebel slaughter which left Jordan's Maria orphaned and violated had an equally brutal counterpart in the Republican massacre supervised by the guerrilla chief Pablo in which twenty Fascists were beaten between two lines of men and then flung over a cliff. Jordan thinks that killing "is their extra sacrament." Loving them, he tries to understand them:

There is no finer and no worse people in the world. No kinder people and no crueler. . . . Forgiveness is a Christian idea and Spain has never been a Christian country. It has always had its own special idol worship within the Church. . . . The people had grown away from the Church because the Church was in the government and the government had always been rotten. This was the only country that the reformation never reached. They were paying for the Inquisition now, all right.

Occasionally one finds a Spaniard who seems almost a moderate, like Frankie Perez in *Adventures of a Young Man*, but the most persistent impression is one of a people who have a history of misrule and violence, and who tragically turn to these very weapons as the instruments of release from their consequences.

GREECE: AN AMERICAN PORTRAIT

George Weller's Greeks in *The Crack in the Column* appear surprisingly like Latins: "Each Greek is a volcano, and when he may erupt no man knows, not even his friends who must quake with him, not even himself." In the number and complexity of their political parties they resemble the French, yet in one way they seem to retain something of the Greeks of antiquity viewing Imperial Rome. Small and impoverished in the shadow of newly-risen giants, they cherish their role as inheritors and transmitters of a great culture. At the book's end, Nitsa, like Molly Bloom in Joyce's *Ulysses*, retires with her reflections:

The whole world is philhellene, as proved by the retreating Germans leaving a wreath on the Tomb of Ignotos before they roared north to die in the ambushes of the Slavs. But most self-surrendering of the philhellenes are the Americans. These young antiques deserve the most utter respect, the kindest care.

FRANCE: A COMPOSITE PORTRAIT

The novels by Frenchmen in this study reveal relatively little about national character and behavior. Stendhal deals with Italians and Malraux primarily with Chinese. However, the ambitious Ferral, head of the Franco-Asiatic Consortium in *Man's Fate* may be revealing. He hopes to make enough money in China to return home and buy the leading French news-gathering and publicity syndicate. With this power he hopes to regain office and "pit the combined forces of the cabinet and a bought public opinion against the Parliament." In Malraux's words one catches, under their cynicism, echoes of the declining power reflecting upon vanished days of affluence:

The threat of bankruptcy brings to financial groups an intense national consciousness. When their enterprises in distant corners of the world are suddenly threatened with disaster they remember with mingled pride and gratitude the heritage of civilization which their country has given them and which they in turn have helped to pass on to colonial peoples.

In *Presidential Agent* Sinclair presents the French as a people who have installed a rotten government to manage their affairs, a government eager to join with Britain in obtaining temporary surcease from German threats to its financial holdings by hypocritically sacrificing Czechoslovakia. They had decided upon "a compromise with Hitler as the cheapest form of insurance." M. Denis admits the resultant loss of power in Central Europe, but consoles himself with the thought that "we still have North Africa and the colonies, and we are safe behind our Maginot Line. Above all, we don't have to make any more concessions to revolution at home."

In *The Age of Longing* Hydie Anderson reports Feyda Nikitin's deadly activities to Jules Commanche of the French Home Security Department. A scholar and hero of the Resistance, he is one of a new type, but there are not enough of them to fill "the sclerotic veins of French bureaucracy with fresh blood." Their effect amounts merely to "the injection of a stimulant into a moribund body." In *The Reprieve* Sartre had presented France as unaware and unready before the Nazis, already bled white from great wars. After another conflict, the patient is almost *in extremis*. Playing the recurrent part of American pupil to European teacher, Hydie listens to Commanche's bitter lecture:

Our last message to the world was those three words which are on our stamps and coins. Since then, we no longer have anything to give to the spirit, only to the senses—our novelists, our poets, our painters, all belong to an essentially sensualist world, the world of Flaubert, and Baudelaire and Manet, not to the world of Descartes, Rousseau and St. Just. For several centuries we were the inspiration of Europe; now we are in the position of a blood donor dying of anemia. We can't hope for a new Jeanne d'Arc, not even for a young First Consul, not even for a Charlotte Corday. . . .

He has told Hydie that the French Revolution substituted its slogan for the Holy Trinity, that the scalpel which excised autocracy from the body politic also removed its soul. The French thus seem to be suffering from a malady which, in somewhat different form, infects the Spaniards, Italians, and Greeks. Their splinter parties, their disorganization, their pervasive political cynicism are a legacy of centuries of conflict, inequities, and colonial misrule. But beyond this there is exhaustion, a vitality sapped by past efforts and a sadness increased by awareness of faded glories.

RUSSIA: A COMPOSITE PORTRAIT

Assessing Russian national character or behavior from the novels presents a greater problem than that found in any other national literature. One must first separate Russian Communism from the Russian people. In the same way one must distinguish the old Russian from the new. And this dichotomy has to be made after the Revolution as well as before it. Turgenev's fathers are hardly more different from their sons than are Koestler's Old Guard from the Neanderthalers they have sired. When Rubashov's old comrade Ivanov is shot, Gletkin replaces him as interrogator. Rubashov looks at the shaven skull, appraising the huge ominous figure in the stiff heavy uniform: "You consequential brute in the uniform we created—barbarian of the new age which is now starting."

The pattern of Russian political behavior which emerges from the novel is filled with more violence, more misery, more oppression than that of any other national group. The dying Stepan Verhovensky described Russia in *The Possessed* as a "great invalid" inhabited by devils and plagued with impurities, sores, and foul contagions. This Czarist Russia is a land in which "harmless . . . higher liberalism" is possible, but it is also a country in which serfs live in incredible poverty and aristocrats live in oriental splendor. Within this social structure, whose opposite ends are separated by an even greater distance than the rich and poor of Italy, the forces of destruction are already at work. The basic situation reveals opposed characteristics: authoritarianism on the ruling level, immense capacity for dumb suffering in the submerged masses, and an intense drive toward a reorientation of the social structure on the part of the militant intellectuals. These factors, on a smaller scale, are to be found in other literatures. But Dostoyevsky also portrays a conflict peculiar to Russia. It is the struggle between those culturally oriented toward the West and the Slavophiles who reject its influence. A Slavophile himself, Dostoyevsky seems to speak through Shatov, who says that the Russians are "the only 'god-bearing' people on earth, destined to regenerate and save the world in the name of a new God, and to whom are given the keys of life and of the new world . . ." This extreme national consciousness pervades these novels, whether it is expressed in terms of a messianic mission or a deep sympathy for a people with a tragic history.

Conrad, in *Under Western Eyes*, made a definite effort to assess the Russian character. He felt, though, that this was an extremely difficult task in which the language barrier was the least of the obstacles which stood in the way of understanding. He describes Russians as great players with words, manipulators of abstract ideas. He feels that in other areas their behavior, like that of Nathalia Haldin, is sometimes almost incomprehensible. His narrator says:

I knew her well enough to have discovered her scorn for all the practical forms of political liberty known to the Western world. I suppose one must be a Russian to understand Russian simplicity, a terrible, corroding simplicity in which mystic phrases clothe a naive and hopeless cynicism. I think sometimes that the psychological secret of the profound difference of that people consists in this that they detest life, the irremediable life of the earth as it is, whereas we Westerners cherish it with perhaps an equal exaggeration of its sentimental value.

Nathalia tells the old teacher that "the shadow of autocracy" hangs over each Russian, much as does its more substantial modern counterpart, the Soviet MVD. Razumov is another Slavophile who believes that Russia is sacred. But later Conrad returns to the subject of Russian incomprehensibility when he says that Western ears "are not attuned to certain tones of cynicism and cruelty of moral negation, and even of moral distress already silenced at our end of Europe."

Koestler's two novels considered here describe Russia after the deluge. The bloodbaths have changed the names and faces, but the same moral negation is there. More accurately, there is not even a negation, for there is no positive assertion of moral values to negate. The doctrine that history has no conscience had removed for the Soviets the need for moral reference points. As a result, they had sailed without the ethical ballast that Rubashov, at the end of his life, decided was essential. In his judgment this was the fatal break in the logical chain which caused the betrayal of the revolution which Mailer mourned in *Barbary Shore*. In this case, perhaps, history is character. The span of events covered by these novels might even be graphed. The line would form itself into two low plateaus separated by a single tremendous peak. This eminence would represent the ill-fated revolt against tyranny. On either side would be the depths in which a people was submerged with not quite passive suffering under a rigid, repressive rule made possible by a long historical pattern and the mass conditioning to obedience which it produced.

UNION OF SOUTH AFRICA: A SELF-PORTRAIT

The Boers of South Africa are presented, especially in Paton's novels, as a simple and stern people who are also good fighters and good haters. Subduing part of a continent and making it their own, they regard themselves as the elect among the children of men quite as much as do the Slavophiles. Yet these Afrikaners suffer from a curious case of schizophrenia. Singled out by the Almighty, they are nonetheless so fearful of the colored population that they repress them as harshly as any European nation ever did its colonial peoples. Early in *Too Late the Phalarope* Paton epitomizes this national group:

they had trekked from the British Government with its officials and its missionaries and its laws that made a black man as good as his master, and had trekked into a continent, dangerous and trackless, where wild beasts and savage men, and grim waterless plains, had given way before their fierce will to be separate and survive. Then out of the harsh world of rock and stone they had come to the grass country, all green and smiling, and had given to it the names of peace and thankfulness. They had built their homes and their churches; and as God had chosen them for a people, so did they choose him for their God, cherishing their separateness that was now his Will. They set their conquered enemies apart, ruling them with unsmiling justice, declaring "no equality in Church or State," and making the iron law that no white man might touch a black woman, nor might any white woman be touched by a black man.

This is a patriarchal society, ruled by men such as Jakob Van Vlaanderen, a political leader who privately calls the members of Parliament "his span of oxen." Fiercely nationalistic, they hate the British, and as they fought them so they fight any force, even a sociological one, which threatens their hard-won supremacy. In the Union of South Africa there are willing British subjects and British sympathizers, but they have not been represented by a group of novels as fine as these of Paton's. This is perhaps due to the fact that they do not form so homogeneous a cultural and ethnic group as do the Boers and their descendants. For another thing, the political star of the Boers has been in the ascendant in the past few decades, while that of the pro-British has seemed about to set as it did in India.

GERMANY: A SELF-PORTRAIT

When Sinclair's Lanny Budd goes to the week-long Nazi Party orgy at Nuremberg, he sees before him a people who have surrendered personal responsibility to a father image quite as fully as did Silone's simple peasants. A people smarting from humiliating defeat had accepted the dream of a thousand year Reich. And it had been sold to them by a man as possessed as any of Dostoyevsky's characters. Roderich Stamm in *Heaven Pays No Dividends* is oblivious to much of the transition that takes place in Germany during the late twenties and early thirties. Through his father's conversations, however, he senses some of the problems soon to be expressed in political action: "They contained the whole uncertainty of our age. There was something intangible and threatening in the air. It had all started with the world crisis and the huge unemployment figures, and then the Nazis had come, and then the Communists." These forces and the movements which they precipitate are too strong for a republic barely fifteen years old. A people used to authoritarian rule reverts to it. When war comes Roderich realizes "we were all involved, because all of us had capitulated before HIM during all these years. We had all given HIM permission to start a war at HIS discretion, when HE decided it was necessary." One is justified in distrusting stereotypes as inaccurate generalizations. But in this case the stereotype is borne out and emphasized in the novel.

Many areas of these national portraits are only roughed in, with the fine-line detail missing. In other places there are gaps. This is partly because some of the groups of novels are small. It is also due to the fact that the novelist does not exhaustively examine voting trends, statistically analyze attitudinal changes, or plot the frequency of government realignments. Sinclair frequently approaches this method and Dos Passos gives some of the raw data upon which such estimates can be made. But generally the novelist tends to proceed from individuals to groups, extrapolating group behavior from individual behavior. This is the method used by Koestler and Conrad. While it does not have the statistical validity of the political scientist's work, it has advantages which complement it. The novelist, with his artistic insight and his ability to shape his material as he wishes, can highlight his concept of a particular national character with drama and human interest to make this hard-to-define quality come memorably alive on the printed page.

chapter five

The Novelist as Analyst of
Group Political Behavior

The economic criterion is one of two means used by the political novel for classifying groups. The other index identifies groups by means of overt political behavior—party membership, acceptance of discipline, performance of specific acts. These two means of classification are not parallel but complementary. The first, in a sense, serves as a background for the second. Although the first is economic, its validity lies in the fact that party lines tend to follow economic ones, that modern political theory, particularly that of revolution, has been based increasingly upon economic facts as well as political ones. The approach of this chapter differs from that of the previous one in tracing behavior patterns which cut across national lines.

ECONOMIC GROUPS

The Lumpenproletariat

In trying to use these indices of group behavior it is no longer possible to deal in general terms such as "the poor." Though "proletariat" may be precise enough for Marxism, even this term is too inclusive for close analysis of the material in these novels. Several gradations are possible within this least fortunate group on the economic scale. Professor Ambrogio Donini's introduction to the Italian edition of *The Pine Tree and the Mole* identifies the lowest group in that novel as members of the *lumpen-proletariat*. These people are not the workers whose taking of the factories Taddei fleetingly mentions. They are the lowest stratum of Livorno's life, the drifters and criminals from whom the Fascists recruited members for their Black Shirt squads. It is their motivation as much as their behavior which differentiates them from the workers. While groups of militant workers are usually presented as trying to better the lot of their whole group, these members of the *lumpenproletariat* seem to be entrepreneurs. Rubachiuchi becomes an *agent provocateur* for the Fascists not to help the poverty-stricken, but simply to help himself. After he infiltrates an anarchist group, he aids in its destruction, not because he is personally opposed to anarchism, but because this is the job his employers are paying him to do. Very often in these novels one encounters Communists trying to destroy Socialists ostensibly because Socialism is thought to be a palliative rather than a solution to the worker's problems. But these underworld figures do not have even this theoretical justification.

Although this group is not nearly so numerous in the novel as many others, its representatives occasionally appear. In *Fontamara*, Peppino Goriano returns to Fontamara after thirty-five years, some of them spent in a "political career" in Rome. A good man, he had been forced by starvation to become an *agent provocateur* for the police. He had earned five lire a day plus a twenty-five lire bonus each time a job resulted in his going to the hospital. For a brief time he had been a hero after a picture of him helping to wreck a Communist newspaper office had appeared in a newspaper. But the "Hero of Porta Pia" lost the honest job he had finally found when it was decided that "fascism could no longer shelter in its bosom such delinquents as had been convicted several times for theft." Pablo in *For Whom the Bell Tolls* is a study in deterioration. A cruel but effective anti-Fascist at the beginning of the war, he is found by Robert Jordan to be a sotted semi-bandit who opposes Jordan's blowing of the bridge. Having lost control of the band to his woman Pilar, Pablo tries unsuccessfully to forestall the demolition by stealing part of Jordan's equipment. Although he leads the retreat after the bridge is blown, Pablo is no longer one of the "illusioned ones." He is a guerrilla who retains only his violence and a dominating desire for survival. Old Zaccaria in *A Handful of Blackberries* is a bandit first and a partisan second. He had received a decoration for a crippling encounter with a German patrol, but the source of the battle was a truckload of cheese which he intended for the black market rather than a desire to free Italy. These characters are not nearly such low forms of life as some of the members of Taddei's *lumpenproletariat*, but they are a part of that group to be found on the fringes of most political conflicts, individuals motivated by desire for personal gain rather than by principle.

Peasants

Almost as submerged in the economic structure is the peasant class. Here too there are extra-national similarities. The *paisans* of Silone and Taddei and the *muzhiks* of Turgenev and Dostoyevsky have characteristics in common. Ground down by oppression and exploitation, they engage in political action only as a result of outside stimulation rather than as a result of spontaneous desire among themselves. Often they may be too devitalized even to do that. When Bazarov in *Fathers and Sons* tells the peasants that they are the hope of Russia, he does not suspect "that in their eyes he was all the while something of the nature of a buffooning clown." In a more subtle way Don Paolo tries to awaken the peasants of Pietrasecca in *Bread and Wine*. He has a little success with parables, but a direct attack upon issues produces nothing. When he goes to Fossa he asks the lawyer Zabaglione about peasant participation in the now disbanded Socialist Leagues. Zabaglione tells him:

What Socialism meant to most of them was a chance to work and eat till their stomachs were full, to work and sleep in peace, without having to be afraid of the morrow. In the league premises at Fossa, next to the bearded portrait of Karl Marx, there was a picture of Christ in a red shirt. On Saturday nights the peasants came to the league to sing "Up, brothers! Brothers, arise!" and on Sunday morning they went to Mass to say "Amen." The permanent occupation of a Socialist leader was writing recommendations.

The American representatives of this class seem much the same. Garland's *A Spoil of Office* follows the abortive political careers of the Grange and the Farmer's Alliance. Bradley Talcott sees this latter movement as "the most pathetic, tragic, and desperate revolt against oppression and wrong ever made by the American farmer." His guiding star Ida puts it even more simply: "While our great politicians split hairs on the tariff, people starve. The time has come for rebellion." Conditions in Iowa have changed eighty years later, but in the deep South they are almost as bad. William Russell's *A Wind Is Rising* (1950) focuses on Negro tenant farmers charged 500 per cent interest by the landowners and cheated of part of the cotton crop they succeed in raising.

Whether he is Prince Torlonia or a Russian noble, the large landholder is most often seen in the novel as the embodiment of the forces which keep the peasant class in subjection. Men like Nikolai Kirsanov in *Fathers and Sons* may attempt to improve conditions, but the predominant pattern is one of exploitation which eventually produces violence. At the end of *A Handful of Blackberries* the peasants kill a bailiff when they invade the Tarocchi pasture lands they believe to be rightfully theirs. Debased and deprived, lacking political awareness, and incited by members of other classes, the peasant group turns to violence. In some areas of the world, particularly the United States and England, a steady economic evolution has tended to eliminate large segments of this group. The Russian peasant appears still to be a peasant, even though he may be a Stakhanovite worker in a large *kolkhoz*. But where the class still exists in a society in which violent protest is still possible, the pattern appears unchanged.

Labor

Commenting on one of the causes of the failure of the farmers' movements of the seventies, Garland said: "They had made the mistake of supposing that the interests of merchant, artisan, and mechanic were also inimical." In the novel these interests are not at all inimical. They are rather parallel, for the labor movement (which includes the last two groups mentioned by Garland) has as its natural antagonist the moneyed class to which the peasants' adversaries belong. And in the novel the laborer is treated as sympathetically as the peasant, with the single exception of Disraeli's *Sybil*, which gives an antagonistic picture of the trade unions. But there are two significant differences between the peasant class and the industrial labor class. The latter has adopted different methods and has met with a large degree of success.

The political behavior and history of the labor movement emerges very clearly in the novel. This group fought its first violent battles to achieve organization. When this was accomplished, concerted action in which the strike was the principal weapon was begun to attain better working standards. In societies in which unions are still free, the strike has retained its tactical importance, but it has been accompanied by progressively less violence. And as strife has decreased, a more effective technique has taken its place. The labor movement has gone into politics. The most overt form of this policy is the formation of a labor party like the one so successful in England. Less direct but still effective is the method used by American unions of supporting the party which seems most likely to serve labor's interests. Peasants' leagues and farmers' groups had been formed to take direct political action, but none achieved such spectacular success as these labor groups. Unlike the peasants, the laborers had to a large extent provided their own leadership. Indicative of their more cohesive and militant nature is the frequently expressed distrust of people in the movement coming from non-labor classes. In *Marcella* the radical Nemiah Wilkins is suspicious of Socialist Harry Wharton. He feels that he is too well dressed and educated to lead a labor movement, and he looks forward to the day when they "would be able to show these young aristocrats the door." Penelope Muff, a dedicated organizer in *Fame Is the Spur*, has the same feeling toward two women who work actively in the Socialist cause. They give both time and money, but to Pen they are outsiders taking a dilettante interest in the poor.

That labor's energies would be channeled into politics rather than violence seemed at one time impossible. Looking back at his youth, Tom Wilcher recalls in *To Be a Pilgrim* that then "the rich men were still boundless in wealth and arrogance; the poor were in misery, and neither saw any possibility of change without the overthrow of society." But the labor movement made the transition from a mob to a party. Pen Muff and Hamer Shawcross had seen it achieved when Kier Hardy, wearing a cloth cap rather than a top hat, drove down London's streets in a wagonette instead of a brougham to take his seat in the House of Commons. And labor remained so conscious of its class origins that Shawcross seemed guilty almost of blasphemy years later when, as a Labourite minister, he wore his ceremonial uniform with its sword and cocked hat. Figures in the novel recall the lines from Browning's *The Lost Leader* about the man who had betrayed his group "just for a riband to stick in his coat." Such a one is Hamer Shawcross. Another is Chester Nimmo. Their supposed betrayal seems more heinous because of this class consciousness. Dick Remington may change from Liberal to Tory with a minimum of obloquy, but when Shawcross enters a wartime coalition government he is a Judas.

When Sinclair published *Oil!* in 1926 he saw the activities of the labor movement almost completely in terms of a class struggle. But it was an index of the relative progress of the American movement as compared with the English that strike violence remained the chief weapon on this side of the Atlantic. Two years later, in *Boston*, the situation was worse. He wrote that Massachusetts had "evolved a complete technique of labor smashing" in which a strike-breaking department developed in the Boston police force was rented out to manufacturers in neighboring towns. He concluded that Sacco and Vanzetti were not convicted and executed for a fatal armed robbery. They were killed because they represented the forces of social revolt to the banking and industrial interests which felt themselves critically threatened. Even eight years later, *In Dubious Battle* represented large segments of the labor group as ill-treated men whose efforts to attain better wages and working conditions were opposed, not only by the employers, but by the forces of the state as well. It is in Dos Passos' books that the American labor movement is seen making the transition from economic to political action. In *Adventures of a Young Man* the pecan-shellers, the miners, the auto-workers are organized as forces which will obtain concessions through direct economic action rather than legislation. But *The Grand Design* shows labor at work within the Democratic Party. There is no nationwide labor party, but the votes of the labor group are marshalled in support of candidates whose programs will provide them with legislative relief.

The continental labor movements, particularly the Italian, are portrayed in the novel as having a greater history of violence and misfortune than those in either England or the United States. Taddei's Socialist workers take over their factories at gun point. Silone's laborers are victimized by The Promoter. Koestler's Rubashov recalls his mission of telling Little Loewy that the interests of his Belgian dock workers were to be subordinated to those of Russia. Similarly, the Fascists had destroyed the Italian labor movement for the purposes of the corporate state. And, of course, the classic irony was the full name for which "Nazi" stood: National Socialist German Workers Party.

The behavior patterns of the labor movement traced in the novel reveal gradual change. A more homogeneous and dynamic group than the peasants, labor has just as extensive a heritage of exploitation and strife. Although leadership has sometimes come from outside their class, it has been provided to a large extent by a dedicated and indigenous elite. Whole national labor movements have been submerged under totalitarianism; others have appeared to be sacrificed as pawns by leaders intent upon personal aggrandizement. But as the movement has matured, old weapons have been used with increasing moderation and new ones have been added to the arsenal. Organs such as the CIO Political Action Committee appear in none of the novels in this study, but such instruments typify the new tactics by which gains are obtained through political pressure. The archetype, of course, is England's Labour Party, which, in assuming national power, has had to make the final transition by directing legislation which should benefit not only its own members but those of all classes of the nation. This represents an evolutionary development which is a reflection of some of the English national characteristics seen in the novel. Perhaps one ends not with a conclusion but with a question. The conservatives and liberals, the Republicans and Democrats, derive their strength from areas which are fairly well defined but which to some extent cut across economic and occupational lines. Can an instrument forged in hottest partisan conflict discharge the responsibility which comes with the attainment of the goal of political power? Can it legislate for a society, or will its antecedents compel it to serve a special interest group?

Proletarians

During the thirties members of the peasant and labor groups were the subject of a literary movement which produced the proletarian novel. This type of novel is generally unsatisfactory for the study of group behavior patterns considered here since its emphasis is much more sociological than political. There are some exceptions, however. *The Iron Heel, Man's Fate,* and *In Dubious Battle* have been called proletarian novels. Other proletarian novels not included in this study were written by Dos Passos, Farrell, Shaw, and Silone. The two novels by Malraux and Steinbeck straddle the line between the political and the proletarian. This is also true of *A Wind Is Rising*, which came after the movement as such had spent itself but which concentrated upon one of its favorite subjects, the southern sharecropper. Some of the proletarian novels have political overtones. Sherwood Anderson's *Beyond Desire* (1932), which was meant as his contribution to the proletarian cause, followed the career of Red Oliver as a Communist labor organizer in southern textile mills. Like Jim Nolan, he is shot to death. But this novel does not reveal as fully as Steinbeck's book the part of the Communist Party's labor strategy in its overall plan. The men of Liam O'Flaherty's *The Informer* are proletarians, members of the Irish Republican Army fighting the British. But in its most common form, the proletarian novel stopped just short of political action. It would present in dramatic fashion the conditions under which the members of this actually diverse group lived. If they took positive action, it was usually to join a union or the Communist Party. Steinbeck's *The Grapes of Wrath* shows the broad scale social delineation the proletarian novel permits; it also shows clearly that though its ultimate aim may be political, its primary textual emphasis is not.

The Middle Class

The middle class is not as well represented as other groups in the political novel. Of course, definition is a problem. In terms of economics, Glenn Spotswood and Robert Jordan are members of the middle class. In terms of politics, however, they are not bourgeois but intellectuals, Jordan a liberal and Spotswood a radical. Perhaps the true middle class does not provide enough drama for the novelist who deals with politics. Most of the people in *It Can't Happen Here* are middle class citizens, but they do not move and act in their normal environment. Their apathy has permitted the rise of a dictatorship, forcing them into the role of the persecuted or the underground fighter. Most often a novelist using a middle class hero will work a transformation upon him in which he changes his class identity. He will, like Glenn Spotswood, cast his lot with the class economically below his. Or, like Harvey Sayler in *The Plum Tree*, he will rise above it through political advancement which brings him power and wealth. In rare cases, the hero will manage to ride both horses at once. Peter Stirling, in Ford's novel, will obviously be a successful candidate for the governorship of New York. But his stepping stone has been nearly twenty years of work in New York City's tenement-ridden Sixth Ward. Ford's style virtually guarantees that Stirling will be neither fish, flesh, nor fowl by the end of the book, but his career too makes it impossible to label him a member of the middle class from which he started. In *The Grand Design* Dos Passos sometimes shows the middle class Washington office worker. Throughout *District of Columbia*, particularly in his prose poems, he refers to or quotes members of this class along with the executives and laborers. But there is such diversity that it is difficult to draw conclusions. Perhaps this difficulty in discerning pronounced patterns is in itself an indication of the nature of this class. Midway between the economic and political extremes, it has a leavening of the characteristics of both. But the political figure who comes from the middle class most often leaves it. If he does not, he apparently has less interest for the political novelist.

The Rich and Well Born

The economic and social upper classes appear in more different hues than any other class. They vary all the way from "red" millionaires like *Oil!*'s Bunny Ross to the same novel's many "malefactors of great wealth." Except for Disraeli's heroes, his aristocrats are very often those usually described as "the product of exhausted loins." Unless members of the English aristocracy take an active interest in the welfare of the classes below their own, they are usually portrayed as despising them. George Meredith's aristocrat appears to hate these occupants of a world different from his. The Debarry family in *Felix Holt* has humanitarian impulses, but its political action is directed toward maintaining its elevated position. Trollope's aristocratic Liberals make efforts toward legislation which will reduce inequities, but far more typical is the old Earl, "Buck" Lostwithiel in *Fame Is the Spur*. A wringer of the poor and accident-maker for inconvenient opponents, he is deterred from horsewhipping Hamer Shawcross only by a raised sabre.

The evil aristocrat is not so common in the American novel as in the English. Mrs. Stowe and Tourgée portray him during the latter half of the nineteenth century in the South. Sinclair's Back Bay Brahmins, years later, take violent action, sticking neither at hypocrisy nor dishonesty, to assert a form of slavery which is more economic than legislative. But aside from villains such as those in *The Plum Tree*, whose power actually comes more from money than lineage, the villainous role is usually assigned to the industrialist rather than the blueblood. This may be a substantiation of the charge that the primary aristocracy of America is one of wealth rather than breeding or cultivation. The Italian noble class is consistently portrayed as an oppressor no matter what the form of government under which it operates. Serfs are freed and reforms are instituted in *Fathers and Sons*, but offstage are the sounds of floggings and the murmurs of oppressed victims. The Marchesa Raversi's Liberal Party in *The Charterhouse of Parma* is anything but liberal. Individuals like the radical poet Ferrante Palla find as little favor with her as they do with the absolutist Ernesto IV. Separated from these nobles by time and space, Malraux's Ferral and his backers have as little sympathy for the Chinese on whom they thrive as does Fabio Conti for Parma's commoners.

There are some good aristocrats in the political novel. All of Disraeli's Young England heroes approach politics with high seriousness and dedication. Coningsby is so suffused with virtue that he keeps his purity unsullied at the expense of losing his inheritance. Tancred's politics are intermingled with a religious mysticism that leads him to the Holy Land. Meredith's Beauchamp is such an emotional firebrand in his radical convictions that he makes Disraeli's young men look like mild and high minded Rover Boys. But he belongs to their class. A little farther down on the social and economic scale is Cary's Edward Wilcher. A politician of entirely different kidney from these zealous young men, he is a sophisticated and cynical careerist who writes embarrassing epigrams about members of his own party. But he is like the others in his concern for progressive legislation rather than perpetuation of the privileges of his own social group. Augustine St. Clare is one of Mrs. Stowe's better slave-owners. He is obviously on his way to salvation, partly through the influence of saintly Uncle Tom, when he is untimely carved by a bowie-knife wielded in a fight he has attempted to stop. It is this accident which prevents him from freeing Tom. Churchill's Humphrey Crewe is an eccentric and fatuous ass, but his intentions are pure gold. He seeks office because he believes he can benefit the state. In *The Grand Design*, Jed Farrington refers to "the Squire in the White House and his big business friends." But it is clear in the book that though Big Business may conceivably have derived some benefits from the Roosevelt administrations, this descendant of New York state patroons was politically oriented toward less pedigreed groups. If one were to compile a balance sheet for this class, however, the villains would far outnumber the heroes.

Good men of wealth are even harder to find in this group of novels than good aristocrats. Disraeli's magnates are the type who in modern America receive awards from chambers of commerce and engraved gold watches from deputations of employees. Elsewhere, the industrialist is a top-hatted advocate of *laissez-faire* economics whose wealth is acquired more through the sweat of his underprivileged workers than by his own acumen. Millbank in *Coningsby* and Trafford in *Sybil* are rising merchant princes who are considerate of their workers and industrially progressive. But either they are ahead of their time or the industrialists who follow them in the novel are throwbacks to a more primitive industrial era. In *The New Machiavelli* Dick Remington's uncle is presented as a reactionary beast. His Newcastle pottery factory produces death as well as cups and saucers. He is as unwilling to install fans that will carry off the deadly fumes from the lead glaze as he is to concede any rights at all to his workers. The Rhondda Valley, where Pen Muff goes as the bride of union official Arnold Ryerson, has more than its share of Welsh women widowed by the coal mines. The management group remains in the background of this novel, but the miners' efforts to obtain concessions which would now seem minimal are evidence of an attitude not dissimilar to that of Dick Remington's uncle. In Conrad's *Nostromo* Charles Gould has justified his decisive intervention in Costaguanan politics by declaring that he was providing order which would benefit the natives as well as himself. Gould's political commitment gives rise to one of the central problems of the novel—the extent to which his soul has been eroded to insure the undisturbed flow of the bright silver ingots from the San Tomas mine. Gould is not the only victim of his obsession. The other is his wife, who is all but shut out of vital areas of his life and thought. Early in the book he gives her his rationale:

I pin my faith to material interests. Only let the material interests once get a firm footing, and they are bound to impose the conditions on which alone they can continue to exist. That's how your money-making is justified here in the face of lawlessness and disorder. It is justified because the security which it demands must be shared with an oppressed people. A better justice will come afterwards. That's your ray of hope.

All of the lobbying groups in the American novels are financed by industrial wealth. Whether the checks are signed by railroaders, utilities operators, or oil men, their purpose is the same: to apply pressure which will gain concessions. And, of course, in many cases these concessions cause a direct or indirect loss to citizens in lower income brackets. In *The Plum Tree* Harvey Sayler uses his power to make an example of one of these men, "the greediest and cruelest 'robber baron' in the West." The lords of Jack London's Oligarchy specialize in the repression of workers with frequent resort to calculated mass murder. The climate had changed by the time Dos Passos wrote *The Grand Design*, but he included the lineal descendant of these predators. Jerry Evans retains a substantial interest in his economic welfare even as coordinator of Roosevelt's War Procurement Board. Columnist Ed James's off-the-record analysis is that

All Jerry can think of in the emergency is to use it to turn things back into the business as usual channels an' we all know that in the southeast at least business as usual means Jerry Evans' business. Of course he has cleared his skirts technically by resignin' from the directorates of most of his corporations . . . But they are still his corporations.

Individuals of wealth in the novel may derive their money from farming rather than industry, but unenlightened self-interest is still the chief motivating factor. This is the case with the powerful ones in *A Wind Is Rising*. Mulcting their sharecroppers, they derive added revenue from convenient prohibition laws. Other Dos Passos characters like Jerry Evans retain their natural roles even within the New Deal. Driving through impoverished Southern counties, Paul Graves is told that "relief is in the hands of the politicians and the politicians are mostly landlords who save it for their own tenants." Steinbeck's Fruit Growers Association serves its own interests in a more spectacular way. After an offer of twenty cents an hour fails to satisfy the apple pickers, the fruit growers use strikebreakers, vigilantes, sheriff's deputies, and then troops to insure a harvest on their terms.

It is curious that one of the American industrialists who approaches goodness should be found in Sinclair's *Oil!* As in his other novels, the industrialists are the blackest of the black, but J. Arnold Ross is an exception. An independent oil tycoon who conscientiously tries to see his workers' point of view, his rapacity is expressed in acquisition of oil lands by varied methods rather than iron-handed labor relations. After his death it is discovered that his business has deteriorated and his assets have melted, partly because of the naval oil lands scandal. But there is also a missing bundle of one million dollars, and at one point suspicion is cast upon his closest associate and friend. The implied moral is probably that Ross's few unsuppressed humanitarian instincts rendered him less able to survive in this particular jungle. The other sympathetically portrayed man of wealth in this novel is Arnold's son Bunny. Like Yevgeny Bazarov and his father Vassily, these representatives of two generations are never quite able to bridge the gap which separates them. Bunny loves his father, but his symbolic rejection of him appears on page after page in which he almost frantically disposes of his share of the oil money in subsidizing a leftist paper or attempting to found a labor college. Sinclair's Cagoulards in *Presidential Agent* are quite willing to weaken France in order to retain the Skoda munitions works. These Frenchmen are blood brothers of Malraux's Ferral, who does not see the consequences of his economic interpretation of current history. The aristocrats and the wealthy are united in the Thornewell family in Boston. Fighting on two fronts, they eliminate anarchists and liquidate a parvenu entrepreneur in parallel actions. Sinclair's judgments of these representatives of the upper class are violent and condemnatory. Sinclair's condemnation is not quite typical of the political novelists who treat the rich, although more of them approach his position than Disraeli's. When one compares the literary treatment of the lower classes with that of the upper, the difference is striking. One might explain this superficially on the grounds of distortion for dramatic emphasis, or the use of ready-made heroes and villains. But whatever the reasons, the majority of political novelists have been impelled to sympathize with the lower classes and condemn the upper.

POLITICAL GROUPS

The second criterion for classifying political groups mentioned at the beginning of this chapter was that of overt political behavior. The political novel describes the behavior of the group to which its characters belong, that group which, while seeking office or discharging it, conforms to a set of rules both written and unwritten. From one point of view, these seem almost like the rules for playing a game. From another point of view, they are the principles which must be followed if what passes for success is to be achieved. And these maxims are not merely empty phrases, for in the novel the politicians who flaunt them fail. An oversimplified summary of their content would be: follow party discipline regardless of any other considerations; use any means likely to be effective to gain an advantage over an opponent; follow political courses which are expedient rather than exemplary. One of the most succinct statements of this attitude is made by Senator Ratcliffe in Adams's *Democracy*:

If Washington were President now, he would have to learn our ways or lose his next election. Only fools and theorists imagine that our society can be handled with gloves or long poles. . . . If virtue won't answer our purposes, we must use vice, or our opponents will put us out of office . . .

Office Holders: Rules and Skills

Trollope's novels constitute an excellent primer for the politician. Phineas Finn's political eclipses are caused primarily by his persistent habit of voting in accordance with his conscience rather than the Liberal Party line. Edward Wilcher in *To Be a Pilgrim* takes what he believes will be a vacation from politics after losing his seat in a close election. When he is ready to return, he finds that his party will not have him. His brother Tom reflects, "Perhaps they were always doubtful of him. They may have felt that he wasn't single-minded enough. They didn't like his writing, especially things like essays and criticism. Just as the Tories never liked Balfour's writing philosophy." When Phineas Finn's friend the Duke of Omnium becomes Prime Minister, he permits himself the same luxury of being impolitic. The death of the Marquis of Mount Fidgett gives him a chance to award the Order of the Garter, normally given as a party spoil rather than a tribute to merit. When Omnium bestows it upon the good, fuddled, philanthropist Lord Earlybird, he nearly deals the deathstroke to his weakening coalition. Mr. Daubeny, on the other hand, is a consummate artist at the game of politics. Needing a vote of confidence to remain in office, he conjures up a seemingly foolproof and completely hypocritical measure for the test. As the head of the Tories, he introduces a bill for the disendowment of the Established Church. He assumes that the Liberals will be forced to vote for it as legislation they might themselves have proposed. But the Liberals play the expedient game, too, with the result that the Tories support what they are against to remain in office while the Liberals oppose what they are for in order to turn the Tories out. In other novels the conservatives also appear just as adept at rough and tumble politics as their opponents. Lord Lostwithiel hires Tom Hannaway to bribe Hamer Shawcross, who is standing for Parliament against Lord Lostwithiel's son. When the attempt fails, Tom defames Hamer by asserting that he has done nothing for his mother even though he has had remarkable success.

Hamer's counterstroke is to take the night train to Manchester, pluck his mother from the happy home she shares with another widow, and exhibit her at a rally the next day to refute the charge. The whole atmosphere of English politics seems permeated by vigilance against quick marches. The wife of a cabinet minister, Nina Nimmo remembers the constant intrigues of groups within that small circle. Quite as wary are the rank and file of the House:

Everything they do is meant to have some effect beyond itself. Indeed many . . . had got so plotty that everything that happened somewhere was "significant" of some "development." If you only asked them to take an ice, they looked at you knowingly as if to ask themselves what you were "starting" and why.

The technique of buying off an opponent is more common in the American political novel than in the English. But the attempt to purchase Jack London's Ernest Everhard is more subtle than that practiced on Hamer Shawcross. Everhard is offered a job as United States Commissioner of Labor. Even though this fee is more respectable than that offered Shawcross, Everhard rejects the offer in order to retain his freedom of action. The ways in which a political opponent can be embarrassed are legion. When Paul L. Ford's Peter Stirling is called out with his militia regiment to protect six hundred strikebreakers, he is ordered to Grand Central Station, the spot where it is most likely that the militia commander will be forced to order his men to fire upon the strikers. Nick Galt in *The Voice of the People* makes the Duke of Omnium's error when he persists in making political appointments on merit. He earns the name of "The Man with the Conscience" but he loses important political support.

"Straws in the wind" may be a journalistic cliché, but the political novel is littered with them. Like Nina Nimmo's hyper-suspicious acquaintances, they are another index of the complex behavior patterns of highly political groups. The ability to sense the meaning behind occurrences which often seem slight in themselves is another talent of the acute politician. When Jethro Bass, in *Coniston*, learns that the postmastership of the small town of Brampton is to go to another's protégé, he realizes that this is the first skirmish in a coming battle for control of the state. His riposte is to take his candidate to Washington. An old soldier, he gains President Grant's sympathies and the job. The invocation of a dusty city ordinance which pushes James L. Ford's Hot Corn Ike and his iron kettle off the corner traditionally marks the invasion of Mike Grogan's ward by reform elements. Willie Stark in *All the King's Men* rightly interprets the attempt to indict his state auditor as the first barrage in an attack against him by resurgent opponents. In *The Charterhouse of Parma* the seemingly imminent execution of Fabrizio del Dongo makes Parma's incumbent regime totter. The Archbishop is one of the very few acute enough to realize that "honour forbade the Conte to remain Prime Minister in a country where they were going to cut off the head, and without consulting him, of a young man who was under his protection."

The Mechanics of Control

The mechanics by which power is attained and kept require mastery for successful execution and close observation for understanding. Proficiency in applying these techniques is as much the hallmark of the professional political class as are the basic attitudes of the upper, middle, and lower economic and social classes. If possible, an opponent is thrown off stride before the race begins. Jerome Garwood in *The 13th District* feels that his renomination to Congress is assured. But he is hurriedly called home to find that control has been wrested from his chief supporter by an opponent who has called an early district committee meeting after taking the precaution of securing enough proxy votes to establish his supremacy. In *Number One* Dos Passos had noted the importance of seating convention delegations nine years before the celebrated controversies at the Republican national convention of 1952. In this novel Chuck Crawford defeats a rival in seating his delegation to the Democratic convention partly through the offices of friends who have influence in the White House. Often the law is scrutinized for advantages lying buried within it. Hank Martin in *A Lion Is in the Streets* is swept into office on a tide of votes cast under his "God-blessed Grandpappy Law." Passed at the state's 1898 disenfranchising convention, the statute set up educational or property qualifications for voters but made them inapplicable to descendants of men who had voted before 1868. Obtaining photostats of the list of these men, he parcels them out as ancestors to his illiterate followers who would otherwise be unable to vote. Countermeasures against a dangerous opponent include the old dodge of conquering through division. When in *All the King's Men* the Harrison city forces want to split the rural "cocklebur vote" of MacMurfee, they see to it that Willie Stark enters the gubernatorial primary election. Of course, if one has sufficient magnetism, he can charm and beguile an opponent out of his path. In *The Grand Design* hopeful candidate Walker Watson returns from dinner at the White House immensely pleased that the President wants him to "take care of his health." This solicitude takes the form of advice for a rest on a ranch in Montana before the convention, "and particularly no speeches."

The mechanics of political success must of course be applied beyond this highly technical behind-the-scenes area. President Roosevelt tells Lanny Budd that he is moving toward alignment with the Allies as fast as public opinion will allow him to go. In a less admirable concern for the same force, Governor Fuller of Massachusetts had denied a last appeal by Sacco and Vanzetti, according to Sinclair, because he wanted the job for which Coolidge did not choose to run. A refinement and elaboration of this technique is used by Senator O'Brien in *Stranger Come Home* when he tries to time his committee's most sensational charges to coincide with press time for late newspaper editions.

The organization of political machines is also refined into a science, particularly by people like Hank Martin in *A Lion Is in the Streets*, who splits his domain into territories and keeps elaborate files, one on promising opposition men who are to be destroyed politically. Methods designed to insure conformity include devices such as the safe deposit boxes of Ben Erik in *The City of Anger* which contain documentary evidence of the purchase of key city officials. Nor is the psychology of interpersonal relationships forgotten. Jethro Bass in *Coniston* always remains silent at the beginning of an interview in order to force the other to speak first at a possible tactical disadvantage. Even the protocol of visits is analyzed in *The Plum Tree* by Harvey Sayler, who believes

there is no more important branch of the art of successful dealing with men than the etiquette of who shall call upon whom. Many a man has in the very hour of triumph ruined his cause with a blunder there—by going to see some one whom he should have compelled to come to him, or by compelling some one to come to him when he should have made the concession of going.

International Communism

Any discussion of group political behavior would be incomplete without mentioning international Communism. Since Stalin's ascendancy over his domestic opponents in the late 1920s, the Communist movement has increasingly become an instrument of Russian national policy rather than a worldwide movement receiving help from the Soviets. Concomitantly, Communism and Communists in England, the United States, Germany, France, Greece, and China have much in common. An indication of the way in which this force cuts across national lines is the fact that nearly a quarter of all the novels in this study deal in varying degrees with Communism. Even though the behavior of this group is theoretically based upon reinterpreted Marxism, it contains definite patterns which relate to Party discipline, strategy, and tactics which seem organizational rather than ideological. One of the primary ones is the prohibition of original political thought outside the limits laid down in the Kremlin. Deviationism is a cardinal sin which destroys Nicolas Rubashov and endangers Rocco de Donatis. In a pious attempt to avoid such error, Dr. Jane Sparling in *The Grand Design* immediately consults Elmer Weeks, head of the American Communist Party, to discover the proper attitude when Hitler invades Russia. Another pattern is the interpretation—and use—of every action not in terms of its immediate significance, but of its place in the overall plan. The strikes of miners, apple-pickers, or pecan-shellers are not local disputes between management and labor but battles in the class struggle to be used to educate the masses and provide useful martyrs. But all the while, the pretense that Communism is an international movement must be maintained. In *Adventures of a Young Man* this view is purveyed to West Virginia miners:

Less Minot got up and said that the American Miners was affiliated with organizations all over the country that was working to overthrow the rotten capitalistic system that kept the working class down to starvation wages with guns and grafting officers of the law, and that if that was being a red, he was glad to be called a red, and as for the Rooshians, he didn't know much about them, but so far as he could hear tell the working class had overthrown its capitalistic oppressors over there under the leadership of the Marxist-Leninist Communist Party and was running the country in their own interests and was ready to help the workers in other countries to do the same.

In *Darkness at Noon* this diversion of Communism from the goal of international revolution to the service of the Russian state is clothed in a theory meant to make it both logical and necessary: when world revolution did not follow the Russian Revolution, it was resolved that the primary task was to preserve "the Bastion" in order to protect gains already made and to maintain a base for later advances. Therefore in each country where its activities are revealed, the Communist Party is found to act primarily in the interests of the Soviet Union.

The use of racial minority groups has not been neglected by the Communists. Several recent American novels have touched upon this subject. The most vivid and powerful is Ralph Ellison's *The Invisible Man* (1947). The book's nameless protagonist flees the South dogged by discrimination and bad luck. He is drawn into The Brotherhood (a euphemism for the Communist Party) and rises rapidly to become "Spokesman" for the Harlem district. Despite appreciable gains he has made in membership, the young Negro leader is shifted downtown. A bloody riot makes it clear to him that the change in the Party line is deliberate. He finally understands the full meaning of his ideological tutor's words, "your members will have to be sacrificed." His break with the Party is basically the same as Glenn Spotswood's. But here the emotional involvement and subsequent disillusionment are much greater. Farrell makes the same point in *Yet Other Waters* through the speech of a Socialist Negro labor leader directed at Communists who have come to disrupt a meeting. In a long passage completely italicized for emphasis he says, "You are trying to manipulate and betray my people. You are no friend of the black man or the white man. You are the cancer of the working class. You are the architects of defeat."

War, no less than domestic conflict, is seen as an opportunity to extend Communism which transcends the immediate national issues. The Spanish Civil War was both a skirmish and a testing ground in which the full extent of Russian intervention was concealed to prevent direct reprisals. In *The Grand Design* Jed Farrington tells Georgia Washburn: "In the shortterm war we're allied to the Squire in the White House and his big business friends but in the longterm war they are our most dangerous enemies." The subjugation of satellite party interests to Soviet interests is made clear in *The Crack in the Column* by Moscow-trained Zachariades, who arrives to deliver his post-mortem on the unsuccessful EAM uprisings: "Our friends want no more premature, independent revolutions. They have Italy and Palestine to think of." Even the details of authorized revolutions are foreseen and attended to. Leaders like Zachariades and Kyo Gisors in *Man's Fate* are made to order. Hemingway's Robert Jordan reflects about the Moscow-trained, bogus peasant leader of the Loyalists, Valentin Gomez: "You had to have these peasant leaders quickly in this sort of war . . . You couldn't wait for the real Peasant Leader to arrive and he might have too many peasant characteristics when he did. So you had to manufacture one." These novels illustrate Communism's diversity of character and tactics and the rigid discipline it imposes upon its followers under pain of expulsion or death.

Analysis of Mass Phenomena

Interest in mass political phenomena is sometimes expressed by these authors not only through action, but in direct analysis and examination as well. Steinbeck's *In Dubious Battle* opposes two theorists: McLoed, who thinks this particular strike is a good one because it will give him a chance to "work out some ideas," and Doc Burton, who serves as the strikers' doctor to observe contagion in the social body. Sounding more like a social psychologist than a physician, he says

Group-men are always getting some kind of infection. This seems to be a bad one. I want to see, Mac. I want to watch these group-men, for they seem to me to be a new individual, not at all like single men. A man in a group isn't himself at all, he's a cell in an organism that isn't like him any more than the cells in your body are like you.

Like Mac, Jim Nolan is a psychologist of mass violence. He even offers to reopen his wound so that his blood will provide a stimulus for the group to attack the strikebreakers. When the strikers are about to mob one strike leader who has bloodied another, he diverts them from this assault to the one he desires. There are other instances in which a specific theory of the effects of violence is used for political purposes. Just as Dostoyevsky's Pyotr Verhovensky has his circle kill Shatov to cement them together, so Hemingway's Pablo had made his townsmen communal executioners of the Fascists: "To save bullets," explains Pilar, "and so that each man should have his share in the responsibility." The basic attitudes behind mass political phenomena are analyzed by some of Koestler's major characters. Both Jules Commanche and Julien Dellatre discuss the ills of France and Western man in general. Their conclusions are very similar to Rubashov's critique of Communist policy. Finally Koestler himself sums up this consistent point of view when he explains the cause of Hydie's constant and unsuccessful search in *The Age of Longing*: "the place of God had become vacant, and there was a draft blowing through the world as in an empty flat before the new tenants have arrived."

chapter six

The Novelist as Analyst of Individual Political Behavior

Repulsed by his party in his attempt to return to politics after the first World War, Edward Wilcher, in *To Be a Pilgrim*, turns to writing. He tells his brother:

No one has written a real political novel—giving the real feel of politics. The French try to be funny or clever, and the English are too moral and abstract. You don't get the sense of real politics, of people feeling the way: of moles digging frantically about to dodge some unknown noise overhead; of worms all diving down simultaneously because of some change in the weather; or rising up gaily again because some scientific gardener has spread the right poison mixture; you don't get the sense of limitation and confusion, of walking on a slack wire over an unseen gulf by a succession of lightning flashes. Then the ambitious side is always done so badly. Plenty of men in politics have no political ambition; they want to defend something, to get some reform—it's as simple as that. But even then they are simple people, too, and it is the simple men who complicate the situation. Yes, a real political novel would be worth doing. I should like to do for politics what Tolstoy has done for war—show what a muddle and confusion it is, and that it must always be a muddle and confusion where good men are wasted and destroyed simply by luck as by a chance bullet.

Perhaps Edward's insight into this aspect of politics has been sharpened by the fact that, despite his immediate denial, he has been hit by just such a bullet himself. But the impact must have been so great that it sent him into a state of shock which made him unable to see that the novel had done just what he said it hadn't. The muddle and confusion are there, and so are the men who rise above it as well as those who are sucked under and lost.

Motivation

It is hard to draw the line between individual and group political behavior. A man may be a mirror or conductor of political forces as well as a discrete individual. His motivation is perhaps the most individual aspect of his political experience. Most of the leading characters in these political novels are strongly motivated. In only a few cases, such as that of Willis Markham in *Revelry*, does the individual drift into politics. The ones who, in Wilcher's words, "want to defend something, to get some reform," are very common. The "something" that Robert Jordan wants to defend is liberty in Spain, so that "there should be no more danger and so that the country should be a good place to live in." Lanny Budd feels exaltation that in his role of Presidential Agent he is helping to defend democracy. The

reform that brings Millard Carroll to Washington is expressed in the aims
of the New Deal, and a similar response on a more emotional level is made
by Glenn Spotswood. Passing the shacks of the Mexican workers they have
tried to help, he exclaims, "By God, Jed, we've got to do something to
stop this kind of thing."

A powerful motivating force which operates on a less conscious level
derives from a man's being a bastard. Hamer Shawcross in *Fame Is the
Spur*, like Hyacinth Robinson in *The Princess Casamassima*, is illegitimate.
Both men are raised by people who try to give them the emotional security
of which their birth deprives them, but their attempts to change the
society into which they were born seem in part due to the feeling that they
are among its second-class citizens. Razumov in *Under Western Eyes* has
been raised, as far as the reader knows, without any family life at all. Yet
he is motivated in exactly the opposite direction from Shawcross and Robinson. His assumption of a counterrevolutionary role is a direct result of his
feeling that his nation and its existing social fabric are all he has. He tells
the well-born revolutionary Haldin:

I have no domestic tradition. I have nothing to think against. My tradition is
historical. What have I to look back to but that national past from which you
gentlemen want to wrench away your future? . . . You come from your province,
but all this land is mine—or I have nothing.

Generations later, another Russian reacts the same way under the new
regime. Feyda Nikitin in *The Age of Longing* has been orphaned by child-
birth and a counterrevolutionary firing squad. The last message from his
father's eyes was one of "unshakable faith in the Great Change, and of
a childlike belief in the marvels and happiness which it would bring." This
was enough to start Feyda on a career whose apex is the listing of Frenchmen to be liquidated after Russian conquest.

The character of Feyda serves to bridge the gap between men like Shawcross, Robinson, and Razumov and those who are motivated by a similar
but much more powerful force—spiritual bastardy. One of these is the
most demoniac of all Dostoyevsky's possessed, Pyotr Verhovensky. He
publicly ridicules his father: "the man's only seen me twice in his life and
then by accident." It would be easy to make a case basing Pyotr's an-
archistic politics upon a partial transference of his resentment of parental
rejection from old Stepan, his father, to Russia, his fatherland. Tony
Maggiore, the hero-villain of *Caesar's Angel*, is called "the terrible child—
the child who had never known childhood." Canon Borda's analysis of
Fabrizio del Dongo's violent behavior is also based upon childhood experiences: "He is a younger son who feels himself wronged because he is
not the eldest." There are also characters like Joe Yerkes in *The Grand
Design* who set out to change a society in which they feel at a social and
economic disadvantage. The houseboy and then protégé of a professor,
Yerkes is eventually led, chiefly by his feelings of inferiority and insecurity,
to join the Communist Party and to work at organizing auto workers. These
activities are a means, though never acknowledged, through which he can

try to change the existing society into one in which he will enjoy a higher status and more prestige. In *The Secret Agent* The Professor's failure in a series of jobs had turned him into a revolutionary determined to destroy the society which had rejected him. Jim Nolan had fought "the system" as a lone, dispirited antagonist. The example of cell-mates had finally channeled this antagonism into Communism, because "the hopelessness wasn't in them . . . There was conviction that sooner or later they would win their way out of the system they hated." Some few individuals, like Disraeli's exemplary young men, enter politics out of a sense of *noblesse oblige*. But more enter from a feeling of protest. Don Paolo's reflections in *Bread and Wine* emphasize the emotional nature of this motivation in revolutionaries:

He had once asked many militant members of his party what had led them to Marxism, and nearly all of them had confessed that their original impulse, as in his case, had been moral condemnation of existing society. He had read the biographies of many revolutionaries, and he had never yet discovered anyone who had become a revolutionary out of scientific conviction or economic calculation.

The pangs of unrequited love are partially responsible for Peter Stirling's dedication to success in politics in *The Honorable Peter Stirling*, just as Frances Motherwell's rejection by Vic Herres, in *The Troubled Air*, causes her to denounce the Communist movement to which he is devoted. Other motivating forces are just as conventional. Such dissimilar characters as Fabrizio del Dongo in *The Charterhouse of Parma* and Jethro Bass in *Coniston* are influenced by the career of Napoleon. The will to power as a basic drive is more clearly put by Old Gisors in *Man's Fate*: "every man dreams of being god." Mary McCarthy in *The Oasis* (1949) labels Will Taub's motivation as basically this when she says that "dreams of power and mastery, far more than its fraternal aspect, were what had attracted him to communism . . ." In some cases, like those of Silone's heroes, the motivation is quite complex. Don Nicola, in *A Handful of Blackberries*, says that Rocco de Donatis "was the object of the clearest call from God that I have ever witnessed." Yet he had become a Communist and left the Church like Pietro Spina in *Bread and Wine* "because of the profound disgust with which he reacted to the abyss which he perceived between its practical actions and the words it preached." Even Spina's name—literally "rock-thorn"—is symbolic of the conflict between these forces within him. The carpenter, merchant, clergyman, or teacher may drift into his vocation through family pressure or pursuit of the line of least resistance. Almost always the politician enters his because of a powerful driving force which is just as likely to be subconscious as conscious.

Moral Problems and Changing Values

Another characteristic of the politician in the novel is the often-met change in values. Basic to this process may be the frequency with which he encounters moral problems. Some may be like Senator Ratcliffe in

Democracy, whose "weakness . . . lay in his blind ignorance of morals."
But usually a choice must be made between that which is right and that
which is profitable. Sometimes it is as clear-cut as whether or not DeForest's
John Vane should participate in the Great Subfluvial Tunnel Road (a
satire on the Crédit Mobilier) which is to run under the Mississippi and
unite Lake Superior and the Gulf of Mexico. Often the politician must
decide if he will check his conscience in the cloakroom while he votes on
a small issue in order to keep his party in power to attain larger ends.
Trollope's heroes usually make the difficult but morally right decision, but
few applaud them. When Phineas Finn votes for the Irish Reform Bill,
Lord Tulla declares, "Very dirty conduct I think it was. . . . After being
put in for the borough twice, almost free of expense, it was very dirty."

A symptom of changing values is the rejection of the constituency for
the capitol. Even the Duke of Omnium begins to abandon the idea of
retirement because "the poison of place and power and dignity had got
into his blood." The career of Bradley Talcott in *A Spoil of Office* is a
classic example. He thinks of throwing up his political life until his renomination is threatened. Then he finds that his office is the breath of life
in his nostrils. Jerome Garwood's comment on returning to Washington
from campaigning in *The 13th District* is that "it's worth all a fellow has
to go through out in that beastly mud hole to be back here where one can
really live." This pattern is bound up, of course, with the problem of conformity. In order to retain the prize, the politician must pay its price.
Hamer Shawcross puts the best possible interpretation upon his own behavior when Pen Muff asks him why more can't be done for the Welsh
miners. He replies that they will do as much as they can without running
the risk of being turned out of office:

I admit . . . that it's a matter of getting the most out of the second best. If all
things were working for the best—why, there'd be no need of politics at all,
Pen. I suppose the very word means not what we want but what is expedient.

The ultimate change in values, of course, is the sellout such as that of
which Shawcross and Nimmo are accused. There are cases too in which
the change takes the form not of deterioration but regeneration. Most of
these are found in vintage American novels, however, in which the love of
a good woman does the trick. Harvey Sayler, Jethro Bass, and Willis Markham all reject the spoils of unsavory careers and don penitential garments
under this influence. The European treatment is much more subtle. In his
cell, Rubashov finds that his interior monologues are really dialogues,
"that there was a thoroughly tangible component in this first person singu-
lar, which had remained silent through all these years and now had started
to speak."

The Successful Politician

The individual who emerges most clearly from these novels is the successful politician. One can even draw a complete profile of his characteristics. And this composite illuminates not only the primary subject, but

also his counterpart. In the interplay between them one sees the essence of that critical phenomenon, the leader-follower relationship. In *The Prime Minister* Trollope ponders these subjects:

> If one were asked in these days what gift should a Prime Minister ask first from the fairies, one would name the power of attracting personal friends. Eloquence, if it be too easy, may become almost a curse. Patriotism is suspected, and sometimes sinks almost to pedantry. A Jove-born intellect is hardly wanted, and clashes with the inferiorities. Industry is exacting. Honesty is unpractical. Truth is easily offended. Dignity will not bend. But the man who can be all things to all men, who has ever a kind word to speak, a pleasant joke to crack, who can forgive all sins, who is ever prepared for friend or foe but never very bitter to the latter, who forgets not men's names, and is always ready with little words, —he is the man who will be supported at a crisis. . . . It is for him that men will struggle, and talk, and if needs be, fight, as though the very existence of the country depended on his political security.

The Duchess of Omnium's discourse upon the tasks Omnium is unwilling to perform is much more an indictment of politics in its worst sense than this comparatively restrained analysis of Trollope's. In much the same vein Meredith's Stukely Culbrett declares that Nevil Beauchamp has "too strong a dose of fool's honesty to succeed . . ." Hamer Shawcross's own distillate of thirty years of political experience is a bitter brew. Dissimulation is the chief element in the formula for success. The politician must be an adept psychologist appealing not to reason and intellect but to "panic, passion, and prejudice." Shawcross cynically adds that if these factors are not present at the critical moment, the politician must know how to create them. The lesson one learns from Chester Nimmo's career is that the successful office holder must be as agile as a gymnast, as flexible as a contortionist, and as vigilant as a radar screen. In certain instances, the politician owes success to what he does not do rather than to what he does. The ultimate in the ossification of faculties whose exercise may be dangerous is reached by the Communists. General Golz reveals his formula for survival to Robert Jordan: "I never think at all. Why should I? I am General Sovietique. I never think. Do not try to trap me into thinking."

Peter Stirling's list of requirements for political success is quite different. Although he mentions physical superiority and dishonesty, his lecture sounds like a naïve version of the Boy Scout oath. He mentions bosses, but his account of the way he influences his constituents suggests Socratic dialogues in Athenian meadows rather than politics in a tenement district of downtown Manhattan. The physical characteristics which he mentions briefly are noted by other authors, however. Nick Burr is a Virginia Lincoln in appearance, while Senator Ratcliffe in *Democracy*, and Senator Planefield in *Through One Administration*, represent the portly and impressive type. Dan Lurcock's acquisition of Willis Markham is based upon precisely these qualities: "Let him get that magnificent head into the legislature, where it would be on view, and there was nothing he might not do with it." This case appears to exaggerate the value of physical impressiveness, but it illustrates the very real advantage which it confers upon its possessor.

The leader-follower relationship can depend in part upon just such physical factors. Bill Dominick, who rules three congressional districts in *The Plum Tree*, cows many of his supporters with his huge, ex-prizefighter's body. Jack London's Ernest Everhard represents this type with the dross transmuted to gold, for he is "a superman, a blond beast such as Nietzsche has described." Hank Martin combines this physical vitality with an oratorical "kindlin' power" which inspires his supporters. But his appeal is also basic in another way. His theme "Divide the Riches" has an attraction for impoverished back country people which is probably more compelling than personal magnetism. The power of Michael J. Grogan in *Hot Corn Ike* has a completely economic basis. From city departments and corporations he obtains the green labor tickets which entitle their bearers to jobs. For each ticket Grogan receives a vote. In *All the King's Men*, Willie Stark's concern for his people's welfare is also expressed in direct action, but he explores psychological depths in his constituents unplumbed by other politicians. He jeers at them as "suckers," "red-necks," and "hicks," then allies himself with them as one victimized by the same city politicians. Losing his job because of these city bosses, he had become "symbolically the spokesman for the tongue-tied population of honest men." His oratory is violent and emotional, full of questions which bring thunderous crowd responses like those of a question-and-answer sermon in a revival meeting. And he buttresses this primitive relationship with tangibles: an overloaded state payroll, new highways, and a magnificent free hospital. But Willie Stark's appeal is not limited to the unlearned. The intelligent but neurotic Jack Burden works for Willie even while he allows his critical faculties full play. Anne Stanton, a governor's daughter, becomes Willie's mistress. Both of these people see in Willie strength where they are weak. To Jack he is a man who lives in and for the present; to Anne he is an embodiment of strength, a man who knows precisely what he wants and is willing to pay the price to get it. Another practitioner of psychology is Councilor Mikulin in *Under Western Eyes*. He enlists Razumov in his service through his faculty for sensing each man's vulnerability. "It did not matter to him what it was—vanity, despair, love, hate, greed, intelligent pride, or stupid conceit—it was all one to him as long as the man could be made to serve."

Political Pathology: Deviates, Martyrs, and Authoritarians

This topic leads directly to a very curious set of political phenomena. It can be described as political pathology. The line between sanity and madness is just as hazy here as it is in other areas. But one can usually distinguish between one man who is intelligently dedicated to a goal and another who is a fanatic. Dostoyevsky intended that all his revolutionaries should represent very dangerous forms of madness. It is obvious that Kirillov, who believes he can become God by killing himself, is insane. The drunken brute Lebyadkin, like the vicious Pyotr, idolizes Stavrogin as a god, while Stavrogin himself is a complete masochist. Erkel is described as a fanatic who can serve a cause only through one person seen as the expression of it. Shatov recognizes their abnormality. He tells the narrator that they would be lost if Russia were suddenly transformed: "They'd have no one to hate then, no one to curse, nothing to find fault with. There's nothing in it but an immense animal hatred for Russia which has eaten into their organism." Even more lethal a fanatic is the terrorist Ch'en Ta Erh in *Man's Fate*. He nerves himself for his first act of violence in the novel by driving a dagger point into his arm. Later, in a state of exaltation, he stabs a fragment of glass into his thigh to express to his companions the intensity he feels as he proposes that they should throw themselves with their bombs beneath Chiang Kai-shek's car. Ch'en develops an almost mystical attraction toward death which he finally satisfies by shooting himself when the attempt on Chiang's life fails. His opposite number is Konig, chief of Chiang's police. Once tortured by the Communists, he declares "My dignity is to kill them. . . . I live . . . only when I'm killing them." Several of Conrad's characters, notably Nikita the assassin in *Under Western Eyes* and The Professor in *The Secret Agent*, are quite as ready to kill for political reasons. Warren's Willie Stark has a fanatical bodyguard in Sugar-Boy, a stuttering gnome of a man who combines absolute devotion to Stark with the satisfaction he gets from driving a high-powered car and using a .38 Special revolver.

But the fanatic need not engage in violence. He appears to channel his drives into actions appropriate to the political framework within which he operates. In *The Troubled Air* Communist Vic Herres calculatedly ruins his old friend Clement Archer. "Because he's a fanatic," explains Vic's wife Nancy, "because he would sacrifice me and Johnny and young Clem and himself and anybody else if he was told it was for the cause . . ." The political novel also contains examples of the Communist who carries his fanaticism intact with him in his journey from the extreme Left to the far Right. Elsie McCabe and Frederick Newman knowingly perjure themselves before Senator O'Brien's committee in *Stranger Come Home*. And it is clear that they have made their allegations against Whitehead with the same disregard for truth which they found useful in their years as Party members. Another of the same species as Dostoyevsky's Erkel and Warren's Sugar-Boy is Spring's Jimmy Newboult. "Knighted" by Shawcross with the Peterloo sabre, he precedes him into each rally carrying it aloft. But with his scruples and acute moral sense, Jimmy represents a mid-point between the deadly Ch'en and Marion Crawford's sugar-and-spice fanatic. Crawford explains noble John Harrington's lack of zeal in proposing to pining Josephine Thorn in *An American Politician*:

He was a man, she said, who loved an unattainable, fanatic idea in the first place, and who dearly loved himself as well for his own fanaticism's sake. He was a man in whom the heart was crushed, even annihilated, by his intellect, which he valued far too highly, and by his vanity, which he dignified into a philosophy of self-sacrifice.

In *Bread and Wine* Luigi Murica tells Pietro Spina, "I decided that politics was grotesque—nothing but an artificial struggle between rival degenerates." His comment may be taken literally as well as figuratively, for political and sexual pathology are combined in the cases of the deviates in these novels. There are enough to fill a textbook of abnormal psychology. The most common is the homosexual who often seeks to achieve through political association the sense of acceptance by his fellows which he feels is denied him by his maladjustment. Such a one is Marcello Clerici in *The Conformist*. Moravia's detailed treatment virtually gives a case history following a familiar pattern. Marcello's feeling of abnormality is deepened by a childhood traumatic experience in which he barely escapes assault by a middle-aged man. Marcello marries, but he remains a latent homosexual throughout his life, feeling a frightening desire to submit when he is accosted by an old man in a situation very like the first one. He hopes to achieve conformity through marriage and membership in the Fascist Party. After paving the way for the political murder of a former teacher, he reflects that the success of the regime is needful to him psychologically. "Only in that way," he thinks, "could what was normally considered an ordinary crime become, instead, a positive step in a necessary direction." This maladjustment is found on many levels, from that of Communist General Ares in *The Crack in the Column* to post-adolescent Winthrop Strang in *The Grand Design*. The son of a famous author now deceased, Strang petulantly complains that he is not receiving enough attention from his dominating mother, a well-known newspaper columnist. In what appears to be an attempt to obtain this affection from other sources, he has thrown himself into Communist Party work and an affair with young Mervyn Packett, another Party member who writes for the Negro press. Lee Sarason, who succeeds Buzz Windrip as American dictator in *It Can't Happen Here*, surrounds himself with strong young members of the Minute Men: "He was either angry with his young friends, and then he whipped them, or he was in a paroxysm of apology to them, and caressed their wounds." The parallel between Sarason and Nazi Ernst Röhm is completed when he is shot late at night by another American Nazi, Colonel Dewey Haik. Several brusque and mannish women appear in these novels. Lannie Madison in *Barbary Shore* is a lesbian who has denied herself everything, including love, to work for the Communist Party. Having broken with it, she is now a completely disorganized personality.

One of the most complex deviates is Dostoyevsky's Nikolay Stavrogin. Although he is capable of heterosexual relationships, he is a pervert who has corrupted a small child and caused her suicide. A sadist, he is also an admitted masochist. In marrying the feeble-minded Marya Lebyadkin he had carried out his idea of "somehow crippling my life in the most repulsive manner possible." In the long-suppressed chapter of the novel which contains his confession to Bishop Tihon, Stavrogin hears the Bishop tell him: "You are possessed by a desire for martyrdom . . ." But the "terrible undisguised need of punishment" is emotionally complicated because this compulsion is a "need of the cross in a man who doesn't believe in the cross—" Stavrogin plays an essentially passive political role since he allows himself to be used by Pyotr. His case represents, however, a combining of abnormalities usually found singly.

One aspect of Stavrogin's character also appears in men who do not deviate from the norm. Nick Burr in *The Voice of the People* looks like Lincoln in his towering stature and his "good, strong kind of ugliness." He prepares himself for his martyrdom by opposing powerful forces in his state, and finally meets it by attempting to halt a lynching. To some, this self-sacrifice carries an almost religious ecstasy. In Moravia's *The Fancy Dress Party* Saverio has been ordered to assassinate the dictator of the South American country of Bolivar. He thinks that he now knows what the early Christians must have felt, "the sweet, deep pleasure of sacrificing themselves for the greater good of humanity . . ." Shaw's Clement Archer and Shirer's Raymond Whitehead do not enter into their ordeals with the intention of becoming martyrs. When they are deprived of their primary sources of livelihood, however, this is precisely what they become. In most of the novels there is an awareness of the political value of martyrs, and the Communists, particularly, excel in their manufacture.

If frequency of occurrence were used to determine whether or not a phenomenon is abnormal, perhaps the dictator would have to be classed as normal. Within political systems embodying the principles of representative government, however, he represents a disease just as surely as a group of cells which suddenly start overwhelming their neighbors. The novel displays not only fictitious tyrants, but real ones as well, from Caesar in Wilder's *The Ides of March* (1948) to Koestler's thinly disguised Stalin in *Darkness at Noon*. The authors usually describe how they act and what made them that way. Since *The Ides of March* uses the diaries and letters of several Roman citizens, the reader learns precisely what Caesar's contemporaries thought of him and what Caesar thought of himself. In the accounts of his enemies, he is a profligate and pervert, a destroyer of liberty. His own writings reveal him as a man who is cold and self-centered but devoted to Rome and possessed of amazingly catholic and intelligent interests. Trying to free his countrymen from superstition, mythology, and barbarism, he rationalizes his dictatorship on the basis that the people will not assume the duties of self-government. He writes:

But there is no liberty save in responsibility. That I cannot rob them of because they have not got it. . . . The Romans have become skilled in the subtle resources for avoiding the commitment and the price of political freedom. They have become parasites upon that freedom which I gladly exercise—my willingness to arrive at a decision and sustain it—and which I am willing to share with every man who will assume its burden.

Like Caesar, most authoritarian rulers appear to believe that they are working in the best interests of their people. Most often this is a rationalization of an enormous drive to personal power, but whatever its source it is almost always a component of the totalitarian mentality. Some absolutists, like Stendhal's Ernesto IV of Parma, make no pretense of extraordinary concern for their subjects. But the modern pattern is for the Duce, Führer, or Father of the People to associate himself with the masses, at least verbally. This is as true of state dictators such as Chuck Crawford, Hank Martin, and Willie Stark as it is of General Arango in *The Fancy Dress Party*. The three Americans also have in common their origins as members of the lower or lower middle class of southern whites. Each starts with a seemingly genuine desire to better the lot of his group. Their careers provide a study of the same infection which attacks the Duke of Omnium, "the poison of place and power and dignity." And this transition from crusader to sick man gives insight into the process by which dictators are made.

Men Behind the Scenes

Another political type which is not quite pathological yet which occupies a position somewhat outside the main stream of normal political activity is that of the silent man, the one who often wields great power but remains nearly concealed from the public. He is found most often in American politics. Major Rann, boss of the Virginia Senate and opponent of Nick Burr in Ellen Glasgow's *The Voice of the People*, "had never made a speech in his life, but . . . he was continually speaking through the mouths of others." Jethro Bass in *Coniston* is another silent man, figuratively and literally. This type carried to the extreme is Dan Lurcock in *Revelry*, President-maker, interstate lobbyist, and national salesman of patronage. A European variant of this type is represented by Karl Yundt in *The Secret Agent*. Described as "no man of action," his function is to goad others into action. This catalytic role is performed by anti-fascist Professor Quadri in *The Conformist*. His specialty is proselytizing the young. Cold and detached, he often channels his converts into actions he knows will be fatal, "desperate actions that could be justified only as part of an extremely long-term plan and that, indeed, necessarily involved a cruel indifference to the value of human life."

The Disillusioned

In *The Age of Longing* ex-Marxist poet Julien Dellatre asks Hydie Anderson:

Do you remember 'The Possessed'? They were an enviable crowd of maniacs. We are the dispossessed—the dispossessed of faith; the physically or spiritually homeless. A burning fanatic is dangerous; a burnt-out fanatic is abject.

With these words he speaks for a constantly growing number of former political enthusiasts who have discovered that they had carried not a torch but a club. One is tempted to call this era the Age of Disillusionment. But this would in a sense be an error, for disillusionment is as old as politics. It is always present; only the number of cases varies. The literary list is a long one—Phineas Finn, the Duke of Omnium, Dick Remington, Hilary Vane, Harvey Sayler, Glenn Spotswood, and scores of others. Even the opportunist Shawcross is not immune. Near the end of his career he asks himself if statesmen are not actually "the true pests and cancers of human society." He thinks that if he could have one wish granted, it would be that politicians would leave all the people alone for fifty years. "We might then have a better world," he reflects. "We couldn't have a worse one."

The modern literature of disillusionment introduces a variation on this old theme. The discontent is localized to one ideology—Communism. Mary McCarthy states one of its basic causes in *The Oasis* when she says that Will Taub's "disillusionment with the Movement had sprung largely from its concentration on narrowly nationalistic aims and its abandonment of an insurgent ideology." In its original use, the term "literature of disillusionment" referred primarily to the body of work of a group of writers who had turned away from Communism. But for the purposes of this study it is just as fruitful to focus on the creations rather than their authors. The best of these novels is unquestionably Koestler's *Darkness at Noon*. It is outstanding not only as a psychological portrait in depth, but also as an interpretation of an important phenomenon. Rubashov is at once an individual and a mirror of forces at work in modern international politics. His journey has taken him from exalted participation in revolution, through consolidation of its gains, to a final questioning of the worth of the whole agonizing process. But his life has been bound up so completely with the cause that even his final renunciation is tinged with haunting doubt. Lying in his cell, one of the last survivors of the old guard, he is unable to repress it:

The horror which No. 1 emanated, above all consisted in the possibility that he was in the right, and that all those whom he had killed had to admit, even with the bullet in the back of their necks, that he conceivably might be in the right.

Rubashov's disillusionment springs from the fact that the light has gone out of the revolutionary movement, that what was to become a new paradise has become an old hell. The dictatorship of the proletariat has evolved into the tyranny of No. 1; the new man has grown into a Neanderthaler. Instead of a promised land, Rubashov has returned from his foreign assignments to find a country where factory workers are shot as saboteurs for negligence caused by fatigue. His conclusion that the regime's error was caused by abandonment of ethical standards is central to the *bouleversement* he undergoes. But even despite this basic departure from Communist thought, it is important to recognize that he is still a Marxist. He even elaborates the old dialectic in prison with his "theory of the relative maturity of the masses." His participation in his mock trial emphasizes the ambivalence he feels. One passage explains this behavior and that of some of the men to whom Koestler dedicated the novel:

The best of them kept silent to do a last service to the Party, by letting themselves be sacrificed as scapegoats—and, besides, even the best had each an Arlova on his conscience. They were too deeply entangled in their own past, caught in the web they had spun themselves, according to the laws of their own twisted

ethics and twisted logic; they were all guilty, although not of those deeds of
which they accused themselves. There was no way back for them. Their exit
from the stage happened strictly according to the rules of their strange game.
The public expected no swan-song of them. They had to act according to the
text-book, and their part was the howling of wolves in the night. . . .

Where there is freedom of choice, the disillusioned one follows one of
three courses: needing an outlet for the forces which originally took him
to the Party, he engages in leftist, non-Stalinist activity; ricocheting violently in the opposite direction, he aligns himself with the extreme Right;
or exhausted, he sinks into a melancholy, nostalgia-tinged apathy. Rocco de
Donatis throws himself into the struggle of the peasants for land. Frederick
Wellman and Elsie McCabe lie with virtuosity in the service of Senator
O'Brien. Lannie Madison retreats into neurosis. The causes of the dis-
enchantment vary. Glenn Spotswood makes his break because he is interested in men as men rather than as pawns in a game. Rocco's point of
departure is the discovery of Siberian labor camps. Both of them, however,
suffer somewhat the same aftereffects. There is a feeling of loss, the sensa-
tion that a platform has been knocked out from under them.

This particular reaction is best portrayed through the creative artists who
appear in these novels. Julien Dellatre is one of three ex-Communists who
call themselves the Three Ravens Nevermore. A scarred veteran of the
Spanish Civil War, he refers to his poems, "Ode to the Cheka," "Elegy on
the Death of a Tractor," and "The Rape of Surplus Value" as "past asi-
ninities." His renunciation of the Movement is complete, yet his tragedy
lies in the fact that he has found nothing to replace it. He has concluded
that "Europe is going to the dogs," that the reason is a turning away from
God, a "loss of cosmic consciousness." Feeling that a new religion is
necessary to save twentieth-century man, he lacks a conviction which
would permit him to take the final step into faith. The great passion of his
life is behind him. In his own comment he has summed himself up: "a
burnt-out fanatic is abject." Another man of letters in the same novel is
Leo Leontiev, "Hero of Culture and Joy of the People," who has come
from Russia to France to address an international peace rally. The death
of his wife frees him to renounce the regime and find political asylum in
France. Psychologically ready to take this step, "he felt as if a whole drug-
store of poison were working at [his synapses]—the accumulated toxins of
thirty years." He has become a Hero of Culture by following the Party line
in literature rather than his artistic conscience. Free at last, he feels that
he must write something truly fine, a vindication of himself that will also
be worthy of his wife, whose death he suspects may have been suicide or
murder. But he is unable even to write the projected *I Was a Hero of
Culture* for the American publisher who has given him a substantial ad-
vance. For him, as for Dellatre, the light had flickered out, and it could not
be rekindled.

Some artists, like novelist Bernard Carr and poet Lester Owens in *Yet
Other Waters* manage to rebound, to continue to work creatively. But still

they bear psychological scar tissue. Even in the process of preparing to leave the Movement, Bernard Carr suggests from the floor that the Writers Congress be concluded with the singing of "The Internationale." And he is moved as he sings. An allied phenomenon is that of the individual who is inwardly in conflict with the Party but remains with it through a fear of these consequences. When Bernard tells frustrated poet Sam Leventhal that he should leave the Party, Sam turns pale. "Bernie, the Party is my life," he replies. "It would be spiritual death for me outside the Party." An even more revealing answer is made by British physicist Lord Edwards. When Leontiev asks him why he stays, Edwards replies: "I told you there is nothing else. You will soon find that out yourself. Besides—once you've invested all your capital in a firm, you don't withdraw it—not at our age, not after thirty years."

The Role of Woman

When women engage in political activity in these novels they are usually cast in one of four roles: man's guide, the reformer, the dedicated Communist, or the patriot. In the years before suffrage was extended to women, one of the few opportunities afforded them for engaging in political activity was to influence or guide a man who was politically active. Emily Harkness performs this function for Jerome Garwood in *The 13th District*. At the beginning of his career he is her intellectual protégé as she channels his reading and thinking. His rejection of this relationship is coupled with his political degeneration and ruin. In *Hot Corn Ike* Molly McMurdo counsels Mike Grogan with acuteness and insight. Since she is a procuress, she supplies very little moral guidance, but her analyses of the factors at work in the district are penetrating if not intellectual. Peter Ivanovitch, leader of the Geneva revolutionary circle in *Under Western Eyes*, preaches the cult of woman as well as revolution. He had been aided by a woman in making his legendary escape across Siberia. The devotion he felt toward her is also bestowed upon Madame de S———, who contributes not only inspiration but also her chateau to Peter's activities. Fancying herself another Madame de Staël, this "Egeria of the 'Russian Mazzini' " appears more like a witch than a prophetess. Possessed of a garishly painted, masklike face whose outstanding features are extraordinarily brilliant eyes and obviously false teeth, she contributes to one conversation by screaming that they must "spiritualize the discontent."

The intellectual guide of man par excellence is Ida Wilbur in *A Spoil of Office*. She remains stolid Bradley Talcott's ideal and teacher even after he has attained the House of Representatives. But she is also an active field worker for the farmers. A pamphleteer and lecturer, she represents the woman reformer who enters into direct action rather than stand once removed from activity. Mrs. Ward's Marcella acts for herself, but to a lesser degree than DeForest's Squire Nancy Appleyard and Spring's three feminists—Lizzie Lightowler, Anne Shawcross, and Pen Muff. Lawyer Nancy Appleyard is a ridiculous figure with her trousers and pistols, but in her feminist agitation she is a precursor of the others. These women are distinguished by conviction, perseverance, and willingness to engage in violent action under pain of brutality and imprisonment to attain their goals.

In strong contrast to Madame de S—— in *Under Western Eyes* is Sophia Antonovna, an influential veteran revolutionary. A striking woman with her gray-white hair and bright red blouse, she is "the true spirit of destructive revolution." Shawcross's daughter-in-law Alice is a direct descendant of Sophia Antonovna. Shortly after her return from Moscow, a letter is published addressed by Zinoviev to the Communists of Britain urging uprisings in the Army and Navy. Implying that Ramsay MacDonald had been pushed into treaties with Russia by Communist pressure, it helps cause the fall of his government. Noting the time of Alice's visit and the intensity of her devotion to Communism, Shawcross suspects that she had helped Zinoviev to plan and write the letter. Dos Passos' militant women Communists such as Jane Sparling throw themselves into Party activities almost more zealously than the men. One of the women in *Yet Other Waters* might be listed under political pathology as well as here. She is Alice Robertson, a nymphomaniac and frustrated novelist whose regard for her current lover does not prevent her from reporting on him to the Party.

There is no Joan of Arc in these political novels, but in Hemingway's book one hears about the fiery La Pasionaria, and in *The Age of Longing* and *Nostromo* the actions of two women evoke mention of the name of Charlotte Corday. In Conrad's novel Antonia Avellanos is as fierce a patriot as her father Don Jose, who had nearly died in inhuman captivity by dictator Guzman Bento. Her fierce anger against General Montero, a modern Bento, is one of the forces which brings cynical dilettante Don Martin Decoud to throw himself into the struggle which leads to his death. She suggests Charlotte Corday to him, as does Hydie Anderson indirectly to Jules Commanche when she asks that Feyda Nikitin be expelled from France. But Hydie's patriotism does not have the fire of Antonia's. She has come to recognize Feyda's brutality and immorality, but the immediate cause of her action is his humiliation of her which breaks off their affair. This gesture is the first positive one she has made. Up to this point she has seemed about to apply for membership in the Ravens Nevermore. Her disillusionment, like theirs, has come from rejection of a strong and disciplined system which answered all her questions and assuaged all her doubts. Her break with the Roman Catholic Church has left her quite as adrift as Dellatre or his companions. And when her gesture fails, she feels herself slipping back into the old despondency, the craving for sureness, for a set of positive values.

Although treated in lesser detail than the men (except for Hydie), these women offer the reader the same opportunity for intimate acquaintance with people who can become more real than those one meets on the street or in the office. Their reality and complexity vary with the skill of their creators, but one is able to follow their actions and thoughts more closely than those of individuals in "real life."

chapter seven

Some Conclusions

In some areas of this study only the main outlines have been sketched in. Good books have probably been omitted, particularly in European literatures. Some mediocre ones, especially American novels, have been included. This was done to give some idea of the development of this form in the United States, but with the fervent hope that a gain in historical continuity would not produce too great a loss through exclusion of more quality. But if a few major points have emerged, this study has fulfilled its purpose.

The press has always been acknowledged as a major factor in influencing political opinion. A close look at the phenomenal success of *Uncle Tom's Cabin* reveals that the right novel appearing at the critical time can exercise wide and lasting influence. With his freedom to place a quarter of a million words between two covers, the novelist can present more information and achieve more reader involvement than any newspaper using columns of factual accounts, brilliant editorials, and four-color Sunday supplements. The novelist can vie with Gibbon and Macaulay if he chooses, ranging freely from century to century, turning from Caesar to modern man, or from Machiavelli to a politician of the twenty-sixth century. Just as the writer treats the rise and decline of empires, so he portrays the flowering and withering of movement. Evoking the past, the novelist can people it with living beings and bring to life its tensions, its climaxes, its meanings. One can gain some understanding of the factors which make men like one another despite national and cultural factors which differentiate them. Silone's peasants, like Garland's farmers, crave enough to keep them sheltered and fed, to give them the feeling that they can work in peace with a feeling of security. One senses differences, however, in political hierarchies. The Prime Ministers of Disraeli and Trollope are masters, but the Presidents of Adams and Ford are badgered servants. There are insights into the small niceties, the little peculiarities that distinguish varying political usages. The American politician's life is exposed to glaring publicity, but the Englishman is spared unless he is brought to court. In *To Be a Pilgrim* Tom Wilcher notes that "Gladstone's missing finger appeared in all caricatures," but "the newspapers never referred to the continuous drunkenness of Mr. A., a cabinet minister, or to even more scandalous liaisons than Edward's."

The novelist is able to hold his subject close or at a distance, and to examine it from any point of the compass. He can slice through the body politic and peel back its layers, stopping to scrutinize the one that interests him. He can follow the early struggles that preceded the English Labourites' rise to power or trace the collateral decline of the Liberals. Even in his treatment of individuals, he can provide a sense of continuity with men of antiquity by presenting modern Caesars. They may dress differently, talk differently, and get their death wounds with bullets rather than daggers. But they are members of the same tradition, followers of the same principles of political action. Nor is the new man neglected. In a sense, Rubashov, with his gnawing conflicts, is as much a new type as is Gletkin with his mentality which precludes conflict. And, of course, one gets much more than history. Tourgée interlards the Reconstruction story in *Bricks Without Straw* with analyses of causative factors. In a long passage he elaborates his theory that "the town-meeting—the township system or its equivalent—in the North and South, constituted a difference not less vital and important than that of slavery itself." Generally the European novelist places more stress upon theory than does the American, but in each literature close examination of causes is hardly ever excluded by concentration upon effects.

The political novel has a well demonstrated vitality as a literary form. The indications are that it will continue to grow. At the same time it will probably display a continuity in the phenomena and ideas it treats. The political novel will continue to chronicle movements. Just as Dostoyevsky and Conrad dealt with Communism's origins and Koestler and Silone with its schisms and apostates, so other authors will follow its eventual destiny. The minutiae of political experience will provide material just as much as the major facets. One example is the "whitewash," the investigation which begins with grim determination and implacable intent only to end with confusing or ineffectual conclusions. Such investigations are directed toward election frauds in *Phineas Redux*, the Great Subfluvial Tunnel Road in *Honest John Vane*, and oil lease scandals in *Revelry*. It is also likely that the political novel will treat a wider variety of subjects. Some of the attention which corruption has received, particularly in the American novel, may well be directed toward other aspects of the political process which have so far been explored little or not at all. The love story or love interest will continue to parallel the political story. But there will probably be more novels in which the relationship will be symptomatic of the same drives or needs operative in the political sphere. This is the sort of treatment given the relationship between Hydie and Feyda in *The Age of Longing*. If one interprets the word "love" loosely, this approach may be seen in the description of Nikolay and Marya in *The Possessed*. The latter novel and *The Conformist* will be followed by more novels in which the author concentrates upon intensive psychological studies of individuals representative of particular political mentalities or groups.

The novel set in the future will probably retain the vitality displayed by such books from the time of Edward Bellamy's *Looking Backward* (1888) to Orwell's *1984*. It is in this area that science fiction may make a contribution to the political novel. Jules Verne's novels were science fiction, but in the society in which he wrote, his work was likely to remain fiction for some time. Modern technology makes it possible for the best science fiction to achieve a greater relevance, to present what may shortly be fact. The world of the future in modern novels tends more often to be a hell than a utopia. And the space ships, robots, and other electronic devices emphasize the godless, mechanistic aspect of modern society which writers like Orwell and Koestler see in it. The better writers of science fiction use this technique. Ray Bradbury's *Fahrenheit 451* (1953), perhaps the best of these novels, portrays a post-atomic war America two decades hence in which technology has been used to kill freedom and make its subjects love their bondage. Guy Montag's revolt against his role in this society may not be completely believable, but Bradbury's three-wall television sets and book-burning fire brigades bring home the horror of a possible totalitarian society of the future with an impact matched only by Orwell's telescreens and Ministry of Love.

The future should bring more political novels than the past because this age is so permeated with politics. The Napoleonic era and the late nineteenth century may have been just as political in their ways as this one, but with modern mass communication media, more people are now involved in and aware of politics than ever before. And, of course, politics has become more complex, more in need of interpretation than ever before. Only a relatively small number of Disraeli's and Trollope's novels concentrate on politics. By contrast, most of the output of Koestler and Silone lies within this field. Each good novelist, no matter what his age, finds the particular subject matter which allows his talents freest range. But his material is life, unless, like James Branch Cabell and others, he creates a reflection of life in a special land of his own which never was in time or space. But as life grows more political the novelist must inevitably reflect this fact, even if only casually.

All this means that the reader who wants to learn about political phenomena from the novel will have a greater mass of material to work with than ever. Overall quality will be at least as good as it has been and probably better as proportionately more good novelists work in this genre. All of the fictional histories, analyses, and interpretations will require the same reader value-judgments as ever. Prejudice will still intrude; partisanship will still distort. But these same judgments are necessary, in a measure, when the reader picks up the book of a historian or a political scientist. And the novelist may use all of the tools in their workrooms while he adds to them his own resources—imagination, dramatic form, and the freedom and scope given him by the versatile art of fiction.

Bibliography

AMERICAN NOVELS

ADAMS, HENRY: *Democracy* (1880). Madeleine Lee goes to Washington to learn about democracy and government. Disillusioned by its state and by Senator Ratcliffe.

ADAMS, SAMUEL: *Revelry* (1926). Fictionalized version of Harding era's corruption.

AMSBARRY, MARY ANNE: *Caesar's Angel* (1952). Rise and fall of a tainted young politician who tries to deal with criminal element in a state adjacent to Illinois.

BRADBURY, RAY: *Fahrenheit 451* (1953). A book-destroying Fireman turns against the post-atomic war regime of a horrific, cultureless, totalitarian United States.

BURNETT, FRANCES HODGSON: *Through One Administration* (1914). Innocent Bertha Amory's husband uses her charm to lobby for his schemes in late nineteenth-century Washington.

CHURCHILL, WINSTON: *Coniston* (1906). Jethro Bass's rise to control of a New England state through mortgage holdings and political deals in the post-Jacksonian era.

————: *Mr. Crewe's Career* (1908). Twenty years after Bass's death the railroads exercise tighter control. Signs of public opinion being marshalled for action.

COE, CHARLES FRANCIS: *Ashes* (1952). Contemporary politics and corruption plus murder.

CRAWFORD, F. MARION: *An American Politician* (1884). Reformer John Harrington's excursion into politics of the late eighties under Marquis of Queensberry rules.

DEFOREST, JOHN WILLIAM: *Honest John Vane* (1875). A weak congressman seduced into corruption by a satanic lobbyist and a money-hungry wife during Reconstruction.

————: *Playing the Mischief* (1876). Attractive Josie Murray gets a fraudulent relief bill passed by a corrupt Congress amidst unsavory Washingtonians.

DOS PASSOS, JOHN: *Adventures of a Young Man* (1938). Glenn Spotswood's development into Communist organizer and his death for Trotskyism in the Spanish Civil War.

————: *Number One* (1943). Huey Long-like Chuck Crawford carries on as Tyler Spotswood goes to jail for him in atonement for his collusion in a corrupt career.

————: *The Grand Design* (1949). Panoramic novel of New Deal and wartime Washington. Conflicts of personalities, ideals, and politics—national and international.

ELLISON, RALPH: *The Invisible Man* (1953). A young Negro's crack-up under prejudice in North and South and disillusionment after whole-souled Communist Work.

FARRELL, JAMES T.: *Yet Other Waters* (1952). Novelist Bernard Carr learns that the Communists dictate to artists too, then leaves despite twinges and "the treatment."

FORD, JAMES L.: *Hot Corn Ike* (1923). Local politics with national implications in two areas of late nineteenth-century New York.

FORD, PAUL LEICESTER: *The Honorable Peter Stirling* (1894). Poor Man's Friend to Governor of New York despite vicissitudes as love and virtue triumph.

GALLICO, PAUL: *Trial by Terror* (1952). Blackmail frees an American conditioned into a robot for a Hungarian spy trial while American diplomats send notes of protest.

GARLAND, HAMLIN: *A Spoil of Office* (1897). Iowans Bradley Talcott and Ida Wilbur fight for the farmers in and out of Congress in the seventies.

GLASGOW, ELLEN: *The Voice of the People* (1900). Lincolnesque Governor Nick Burr fights a corrupt organization and meets his death in post-Reconstruction Virginia.

HEMINGWAY, ERNEST: *For Whom the Bell Tolls* (1943). Conflict of ideologies in Spain as anti-Fascist, non-Communist Robert Jordan dies fighting for what he believes in.

JAMES, HENRY: *The Princess Casamassima* (1886). Suicide frees displaced Hyacinth Robinson from serving London revolutionaries whose cause he no longer supports.

LANGLEY, ADRIA LOCKE: *A Lion Is in the Streets* (1945). Another Huey Long novel.

LEWIS, SINCLAIR: *It Can't Happen Here* (1936). The horrors of a Fascist America.

LONDON, JACK: *The Iron Heel* (1908). America under the Fascist Oligarchy seen in retrospect from the 26th century when near-Utopia is well-established.

McCARTHY, MARY: *The Oasis* (1949). The founding of a seemingly successful utopian colony which begins to wither from lack of feeling of relevance and conviction.

MAILER, NORMAN: *Barbary Shore* (1951). A special revolutionary socialism to be saved for "the day" is passed from one to another of a group of weird characters.

MASTERS, EDGAR LEE: *Children of the Market Place* (1922). Spirited biography and defense of Stephen A. Douglas set against a growing America by a shadowy narrator.

MANCHESTER, WILLIAM: *City of Anger* (1953). A series of tragedies growing out of the "numbers racket" and corruption in a city that looks and sounds like Baltimore.

PHILLIPS, DAVID GRAHAM: *The Plum Tree* (1905). Harvey Sayler gains control of a huge lobby and becomes a President-maker before disillusionment sets in.

RUSSELL, WILLIAM: *A Wind Is Rising* (1950). On the fringes of the political novel. Negro sharecroppers dominated by a hostile socio-political economic system.

SHAW, IRWIN: *The Troubled Air* (1951). One man crushed between self-appointed judges and unscrupulous Communists in a fight against blacklists and guilt by association.

SHELLABARGER, SAMUEL: *Prince of Foxes* (1947). Running duel of wits and weapons between Borgia and one of his captains. Melange of romance, swordplay, and politics.

SHIRER, WILLIAM L.: *Stranger Come Home* (1954). A radio commentator and a Foreign Service career man are ruined by Senator O'Brien and perjured testimony.

SINCLAIR, UPTON: *Oil!* (1926). The making of a millionaire radical, son of an oil tycoon destroyed by oil scandals in the Harding era he helped to create.

———: *Boston* (1928). Defense of Sacco and Vanzetti with admixture of fiction.

———: *Presidential Agent* (1945). Everybody's confidante, Lanny Budd helps make and interpret modern political history up to and through Munich.

STEINBECK, JOHN: *In Dubious Battle* (1936). A glimpse of Communist aims and methods in organizing and directing strike violence for Party purposes.

STOWE, HARRIET BEECHER: *Uncle Tom's Cabin* (1852). The most effective political instrument in the history of the novel.

TOURGÉE, ALBION W.: *A Fool's Errand* (1879). A Northerner tries to buck the tide of a resurgent South during Reconstruction. Acute criticism of the Federal program.

———: *Bricks Without Straw* (1880). More of the same with greater violence and more analysis of the political structure of the pre-war and post-war South.

WARREN, ROBERT PENN: *All the King's Men* (1946). The hectic life and violent death of a Southern dictator with sharp portraits of his effect upon those around him.

WELLER, GEORGE: *The Crack in the Column* (1949). An American flier is introduced to global politics as Communist Greeks fight the British during World War II.

WHITLOCK, BRAND: *The 13th District* (1902). The progressive moral and political decline of a midwestern moth fascinated by the illuminated capitol dome.

WILDER, THORNTON: *The Ides of March* (1948). Caesar's career through Roman eyes.

ENGLISH NOVELS

CARY, JOYCE: *To Be a Pilgrim* (1942). Fading Tom Wilcher recreates turn of the century politics for his niece as he tries to perpetuate the old solid values.

———: *Prisoner of Grace* (1952). Chester Nimmo's 30-year rise from lay preacher to cabinet minister through determination, astuteness, and a political sixth sense.

CONRAD, JOSEPH: *Nostromo* (1904). The rise and fall of Costaguanan governments with help from a British mine-owner who ends up owned by his mine.

———: *The Secret Agent* (1907). Informer Adolf Verloc schemes to blow up the Greenwich Observatory for a foreign power wanting to prod the British into repression.

———: *Under Western Eyes* (1910). A monarchist Russian is destroyed by chance involvement in revolutionary acts. The work of Red circles in and out of Russia.

DISRAELI, BENJAMIN: *Coningsby* (1844). Enlightened nobleman at last becomes an M.P.

———: *Sybil* (1845). A less harried Young Englander does the same. Panorama of England c. 1837–1852 with great popular uprisings emphasizing national discontent.

———: *Tancred* (1847). The hero recoils from politics, finding spiritual and political insights amidst comic opera imbroglios in the deserts of the Holy Land.

ELIOT, GEORGE: *Felix Holt, the Radical* (1866). Provincial politics in the 1830s. Gallery of types from the extreme radical to granite conservative. Complicated plot.

FORSTER, E. M.: *A Passage to India* (1924). Personal tragedies emphasize national tragedy of divided and unhappy India governed by inflexible and unfeeling Britain.

HUXLEY, ALDOUS: *Brave New World* (1932). A totalitarian world of the future in which stability has been achieved through destruction of freedom and the soul.

MAUGHAM, SOMERSET: *Then and Now* (1946). Niccolo Machiavelli learns more about his profession negotiating with Borgia. Time out for dalliance and teaching a novice.

MEREDITH, GEORGE: *Beauchamp's Career* (1876). A fiery young radical's political excursions end in family disruption, failure, and death. More portraits of types.

ORWELL, GEORGE: *1984* (1949). Chilling world of the future in which the regime can control past and present, literally make two and two equal five for its slaves.

SPRING, HOWARD: *Fame Is the Spur* (1940). Over sixty years of British politics with emphasis on the rise of the Labor Party and the kinds of men who made it.

TROLLOPE, ANTHONY: *Phineas Finn* (1869). The education of a young Liberal in Commons. Disraeli v. Gladstone under other names. Phineas's conscience politically expensive.

————: *Phineas Redux* (1874). More of the same with a murder trial added.

————: *The Prime Minister* (1876). The three-year tenure of the Duke of Omnium's coalition. The Duke, like Phineas, now infected by the virus of disillusionment.

WARD, MRS. HUMPHREY: *Marcella* (1894). Liberals v. Conservatives as the scales drop from Venturist Marcella's eyes leading her from bad Wharton to good Raeburn.

WELLS, H. G.: *The New Machiavelli* (1910). An illicit affair destroys Dick Remington as Parnell had been destroyed. Early 20th century political currents.

ITALIAN NOVELS

MORAVIA, ALBERTO: *The Conformist* (1951). Marcello Clerici's attempt to escape abnormality leads him to a career in the Fascist secret police and political murder.

————: *The Fancy Dress Party* (1952). Political and amorous intrigue involving a South American dictator, his secret police, and revolutionaries. Ends in murder.

SILONE, IGNAZIO: *Fontamara* (1934). Growing political awareness and resistance to Fascism destroy a poor village. Peasants v. landowners and the regime. An appeal.

————: *Bread and Wine* (1937). A revolutionary torn between Communism and religion. Pietro Spina seeks the best of the two while underground from the Fascists.

————: *A Handful of Blackberries* (1953). Rocco de Donatis' post-war break with Communism, his survival of its attack, and his re-entry into pro-peasant activity.

TADDEI, EZIO: *The Pine Tree and the Mole* (1945). The top and bottom strata of Livorno society as Fascism uses the underworld to aid in its rise to power.

FRENCH NOVELS

MALRAUX, ANDRÉ: *Man's Fate* (1934). Attempted Communist coup in Shanghai in 1927.

SARTRE, JEAN-PAUL: *The Reprieve* (1945). Many strata of French society during the ten weeks ending with Munich agreement. Impact on them and other Europeans.

STENDHAL, MARIE-HENRI: *The Charterhouse of Parma* (1839). Careers of Fabrizio del Dongo, his aunt and her lover, Minister to Prince of Parma in and after Napoleonic era.

GERMAN NOVELS

KAUFMAN, RICHARD: *Heaven Pays No Dividends* (1951). The rise and fall of Hitler's Reich seen through the eyes of a German reluctantly drawn into Nazism.

KOESTLER, ARTHUR: *Darkness at Noon* (1941). Superb account of the destruction of one of the Bolshevik old guard, with penetrating analysis of his life and conflicts.

————: *The Age of Longing* (1951). Disillusioned Europeans under Russia's threatening shadow await atomic destruction through conflict of East and West.

RUSSIAN NOVELS

DOSTOYEVSKY, FYODOR: *The Possessed* (1872). Deranged revolutionaries bring destruction and death to a provincial city in a book meant to show the danger they represent.

TURGENEV, IVAN: *Fathers and Sons* (1862). Two generations separated by ideas and ideologies. Nihilist prototype dies unyielding as his pupil accepts the old order.

SOUTH AFRICAN NOVELS

PATON, ALAN: *Cry, The Beloved Country* (1948). A poignant double tragedy arising out of political, economic, and social repression of the Black population by Whites.

————: *Too Late the Phalarope* (1953). The personal tragedy of a hero destroyed by lack of understanding and repressive racial legislation for white supremacy.

SUGGESTED READING

CROSSMAN, RICHARD (ed.): *The God That Failed* (1950). Writers Arthur Koestler, Ignazio Silone, Richard Wright, André Gide, Louis Fischer, and Stephen Spender discuss the events in their lives which led them to Communism and the factors which caused them to break with it. An extremely valuable book.

67-3857